MW00749576

"Because things are the way they are,
things will not stay the way they are."

~ Bertolt Brecht

1

Other Books by Bill Engleson

Like a Child to Home (Friesen Press 2013)

Confessions
of an Inadvertently Gentrifying Soul

Bill Engleson

Silver Bow Publishing
Box 5 – 720 – 6th Street,
New Westminster, BC
V3C 3C5   CANADA

Copyright © 2016 Silver Bow Publishing
Cover Photo: Wilf Ratzburg
Layout/Design: Candice James

All rights reserved including the right to reproduce or translate this book or any portions thereof, in any form.

ISBN 978-1-927616-22-2

Library and Archives Canada Cataloguing in Publication

Engleson, Bill, author
    Confessions of an inadvertently gentrifying soul / Bill Engleson.

ISBN 978-1-927616-22-2 (paperback)

    I. Title.

PS8609.N56C65 2016   C814.6   C2016-904428-9

Silver Bow Publishing
Box 5 - 720 Sixth St.,
New Westminster, BC
CANADA V3L 3C5

Email: info@silverbowpublishing.com

Website: www.silverbowpublishing.com
Website: http://www.alibris.com/stores/silverbow

Introduction

More than a decade ago, shortly after moving to my small paradise, I conceived of writing a series of articles on gentrification. This was sometime after I began to keep a journal, not entirely inaccurately entitled, *Memoirs of a Rural Sissy*. After a little more than a year of journaling, I found that vehicle slowly sputtering to a halt. It may have been how my life was unfolding but the days began to seem similar. Additionally, my rural skill set stayed remarkably dormant.

Actually, even before the reactive conception of my gentrification disclosure, I had written a couple of articles about my wayward and reprehensible gentrification instincts and other odd sundry behavior without actually realizing that they were 'confessions of my anything-but-innocent-aging-fellow-gentrification ways.

Since then, a swack of these articles have appeared in the *Flagstone*, Denman Island's monthly journal. The fact that the articles have appeared out of sequence, with an obscure connection, on occasion, to gentrification, though it disturbs me, really only speaks to my occasionally selective, often disorganized mind. Writing to no deadline, I submitted each of them when they seemed ready to be read. The first of this series has remained unpublished until now. The rest follow in order of the first scribble, as true as possible to their original date of conception. Sadly, more than half of my articles' siblings stumbled out of the gate, became mired in the boggy muck of my lost inspiration, and were left to rot on the vine of mixed metaphors and sloth. As you will no doubt notice, I use an abundance of quotes to break up the monotony of my ideas. Sometimes they actually relate to the opinions expressed. Sometimes not! In the first chapter, I begin with a lengthy quote and then settle in to the sound of my own voice.

These writings have had a tortuous birth for reasons I simply cannot fathom. I hope they bring you pleasure and I also hope they amuse.

And, to my good friend and beta reader, Mary McDonough, my heartfelt thanks.

~ Bill Engleson, Denman Island, May, 2016

Table of Contents

The Lost and Then Found

"By the end of the 1990's, gentrification(*) was under way in what had been the most dilapidated and abused districts of Manhattan. Again, the poor, evicted or priced out by the higher costs of renovating, were victims. Affordable housing could have been added as infill in parking lots and empty lots if government had been on its toes, and if communities had been self- confident and vigorous in making demands, but they almost never were. Gentrification benefited neighborhoods, but so much less than it could have if the displaced people had been recognized as assets worth retaining. Sometimes when they were gone their loss was mourned by gentrifiers who complained that the community into which they had bought had become less lively and interesting." ~ *Jane Jacobs, DARK AGE AHEAD.*

Late in life, a time of tardy, slightly muted self-awareness, I am struck with the difficult to swallow notion that I might actually be the epitome of gentrification. My partner, shattered by this revelation, exclaims, "No, no, say it ain't so sweetie. You're better than that! We're better than that! Surely!" She, incontestably, is. Alas, I may not be.

I have always been dimly aware of the scourge of the gentry. With an often deserved reputation as heartless urban exploiters, they infiltrate neighborhoods in decline, commit reprehensible acts of social clear-cutting, renovate till the cows come home *(or until those shell-shocked bovines lose their limited sense of direction under the unremitting radiation of acres of new home lighting, blazing down on their shriveled-up pastures.)* Ravenous urbanites, swallowing land whole with the restraint of a tsunami, engage in chronic up-scaling and shape-shifting, altering whatever stands in their way. Wherever they go, they bring their high-falutin', bull-dozing, over-priced ways, putting on airs, enriching their portfolios, sprucing every blessed little thing up.

I probably should have gleaned that I was one of them. I stem from farming stock, salt of the stump-farm folk, who brought their dispossessed rural hearts to a big city at the tail end of WW2. Initially, my beloved parents lived isolated lives in abandoned mansions, denuded into over-crowded rooming houses.

Subsequently, unsettled by the agitating pace of big city post-war Vancouver, they set to sea in a fishing vessel not much bigger than a soap dish. This attempt to curtail our ancestral inclination to socially stratify, while admirable, may have only subsumed us more deeply into the gentrifrying pit: Life on a tiny fish boat, no bigger than the proverbial sardine can, will cause even the most recalcitrant gentrifier to tease themselves with tiny dreams of self-improvement.

Eventually, we left the sea and plunked down roots on land. The first house my father bought in Nanaimo was a partially completed structure. The previous owner may have sensed that he was a latent, raging gentrifier, *(although in those days, the post-civil war Americanism, 'carpetbagger', was the favoured invective)* and he, reportedly, fled crazily into the dark mysterious hills of nearby Mount Benson. My folks bought his abandoned house for a song. Dad completed the house and we lived there for the better half of a decade.

A large part of what drove my parents was a desire to improve their lives. Inherent in this quest was dissatisfaction with their past lives and a simple wish to improve their station. As younger people, they had packed their bags and lit out to seek fame, fortune, and survival. As middle-ageing parents, with two high needs children, they resorted to using their common sense and their wits to better themselves. But they paid a price. My father in particular had moved away from a large, carnivorously religious extended family in Southern Alberta. His pioneer trek to the west coast meant losing contact with a shared heritage that was sixty years in the making.

Dislocation from place is one common price newcomers from anywhere must be prepared to pay. It is also a good reason for the recently arrived gentry, those newcomers who brazen change and move into your bailiwick, to be embraced. They may not know how to be neighborly the way people in their adopted community practice the rituals of neighborliness; they will need time and patience to learn. The complexities of recycling and conservation are often foreign to them. Their pampered urban lives have not readied them for the rigors of rural responsibility.

As for my parents, their transient wheels came off, and, one move later, they stalled in some form of post-gentrification limbo *(defined primarily by finally becoming content with their life.)* It was left up to me to heed our families gentrifying urges.

I moved away from home to attend university, staying, for brief semester spells, in a series of neighborhoods. Never once was I accused of improving or adjusting them. Just one time I wanted some homeowner to confront me on the street and rebuke me for bringing new-fangled ways to the block. Never happened. It was as if I was a cipher. Students can be like that you know. Unless they throw-up on your lawn, burn the Prime Minister in effigy, streak your tennis match or date your daughter, it's like they were never there.

The years went swiftly by and my awareness of my gentrifying predisposition began to dim.

However, in time, the city I lived in, incognito-like, began to press in, like I was trapped in some grotesque cake of extra firm tofu. In a gentrifying frenzy, a group of friends and I bought a little cabin on Mayne Island. In a fanciful coincidence, we discovered that Bob, our neighbor on Mayne, who was also our real estate agent, and the developer of the small subdivision we had moved into *(in that occasional weekend sort of insidious way many of us ingratiate our urban carcasses into the fabric of the Gulf Islands)* had once rented a room in the very home in the city where my friends and I communed. In Bob's day, however, it had been just a squalid rooming house, not unlike the ones my parents had fled from after the war. Bob just shook his head and said way too many times, "Well don't that beat all?" Bob proved to be a good neighbour however and our shared roots, which we unhesitatingly dredged up most times we saw Bob, seemed to help keep us in his good books.

Bob was so taken with us in fact that for a number of years he even loaned us his old dog, Beauregard, to help us acclimatize to Island ways. Beau knew all the good trails on Mayne and we spent many a weekend taking his lead as he aimlessly wandered all over the bush looking for whatever dogs on the prowl look for. It was a wonderful introduction to Island life I must say.

This, incidentally, might be a generous means by which the gentrifried* can welcome gentrifiers into their midst. If your pooches are willing, consider having the newcomers care for them for a time. What a wonderfully accepting gesture that would be. Sort of a *'welcome wagging'*.

But I was still, at heart, a city feller. We bought a fixer-upper in a neighborhood that had been under the threat of expanded freeways and higher density for over three decades. From the late 1920's, this same house had essentially been a boarding home. WW2 saw the various living rooms converted into additional living quarters to answer a housing shortage.

We spruced up our ninety-year-old home to suit our needs. Interestingly, the previous owner had lived there from the end of WW2, *(the house having been returned to its single family glory by then)* and raised eight kids. We had but two cats and a mother-in-law *(who had her own spacious basement suite)* and often felt hard put for sufficient space.

We've owned land on Denman for almost a decade, residing here full time for almost six years. Burdened with the multigenerational, double-barreled guilt of carrying not only the curse of persistent gentrification *(the inexpungable sin of always being a newcomer)* and, as well, the remains of my once transient, departed parent's dreams, I am compelled to yet again compulsively, perpetually, seek comfort in the welcoming bosom of a new community.

Even if the dogs of Denman have better sense than to be loaned out to me, a more or less complete stranger, I will painstakingly notch my way, weave my way into the complex fabric of this Island community. Eventually, I hope to fall into step with the beautiful, magical tenor of Denman, gentry baggage and all.

---

* gentrifried. A condition common amongst those who refuse to appreciate the newbie's inherent qualities; may also refer to the social sizzling that occurs when the gentry move from the frying pan into the fire.

Pick of the Litter - A Rumination

"There was generally twice the number of food and beverage containers and confectionary items in rural areas compared to urban areas." ~ **PEI Roadside Litter Survey 2002.**

Before I moved to Denman Island, I lived an urban existence. So urban in fact that the nearest 7-11 was but two blocks away. I mention 7-11, not to belittle such a colossally relevant company, but because my strongest memories of the city are the unrelenting layers of litter that clog the greenery, edge the asphalt and swirl in the air when, depending on the season, warm or chilly gusts of smog-smacked wind tornado through the hapless streets. Litter is one of the given realities of urban life. Not only are the streets and sidewalks pretty much inundated with the trashy discards of careless city dwellers, if you didn't know any better, you'd think the paramount rite of passage in the concrete jungle is to maximize personal litter.

While not the only source of street refuse by any means, stores like 7-11 cater to the concept of quick and unremitting 24-7 consumerism. I sometimes call it gulp and chuck. It's a simple precept really. An object of consumable desire is identified, acquired, denuded of its irritatingly unnecessary wrapping, and swallowed whole. The wrapping, as if a painful remembrance of gluttony gone berserk, is tossed out the window or dismissed onto the street.

But the country is apparently not immune from the urban ethos that the whole earth is one big garbage dump. Often I ride my twenty-year-old bike into downtown Denman, usually to make small purchases and pay my respects to anyone I chance to meet. As I wheel back home along Denman Road towards the Lacon turnoff and beyond, I have begun to notice increasing amounts of turfed trash. Bags, food wrappings and other assorted paper and plastic products have taken up residence in and near the gully that twins the roadway. I am saddened and cannot comprehend what would possess anyone to deposit their excess residue on our little country lanes. Don't people own garbage cans? Can't they keep a small plastic bag hanging from their rear-view mirror?

To understand the rocketing explosion of projectile debris a whit better, I began a quick but exhaustive study on litter-bugging.

The term 'litterbug' appears to have been coined by cartoonist Amelia Opdyke "Oppy" Jones in 1947 for use in anti-littering advertisements promoted by the New York City Department of Sanitation. As I was born in 1947, that may explain in part why I am drawn to an examination of this baby boomer era phenomenon. Post-war productivity and the resulting surge in consumer products are inextricably linked to the boomers. It's not necessarily our fault however. Our parents simply wanted us to have what they could not. My parents had little in the way of possessions growing up so there was much to make up for. Still, they managed to demonstrate a restrained capacity to acquire meaningless products which I like to think carried on to me.

My shopping habits aside, most everything in our wholesale and retail world is packaged, wrapped and covered with layer after layer of plastic, paper, cardboard and Styrofoam skin.

As I ruminate on the awfulness of litterbugs, I am also cognizant that they have some redeeming graces. If nothing else, they serve to heighten our concern for the environment. Litterbugs make the escalating accumulation of in-our-face trash obvious.

Rarely are littering laws enforced. On Denman, there is a $2000 fine if convicted. But who is ever convicted. Or arrested? Or cautioned? And who, pray tell, are the litter police? It may be safe to say that most people consider littering to be a character flaw, like nose picking or some other unsightly, unhygienic activity. Nobody likes a litterbug. They clearly are lazy. How difficult is it to find and use a garbage can? It must be that we make excuses for litterers. Their offense is so pathetic that we give them a pass. Poor souls, if that's the worst thing they do in their lives, well, let's be thankful they don't appear to have the gumption for bigger crimes. Still we scorn them.

This is reinforced in popular culture. For example, Arlo Guthrie brilliantly lampooned the Draft via a littering conviction in the movie "Alice's Restaurant". Placed on the group W bench for not being "moral enough to join the army," he is interrogated about his past criminal history by one of his bench mates:

"Kid, whad'ya get?" I said, "I didn't get nothing. I had to pay $50 and pick up the garbage." He said, "What were you arrested for, kid?" And I said, "Littering." And they all moved away from me on the bench there and the hairy eyeball and all kind of mean nasty things, till I said, "And creating a nuisance." And they all came back, shook my hand, and we had a great time on the bench, talking about crime..."

In Arlo's defense, he is clear in his little tale that he at least attempted to deposit his leavings at the dump. Finding it closed, he spiraled down into the sordid world of litter-bugging.

I offer up no solutions to needless litter. God knows whole movements and industries have evolved to combat its spreading proliferation. And just to set the record straight, so you know I'm not without my own littering baggage, I offer a confession. Somewhere in Saskatchewan, in the summer of 1969, in a small town whose name I cannot recall *(except it had a drive-in movie theater featuring The Green Slime, a piece of cinematic litter I more than likely would have really enjoyed),* I littered in a big way. A travelling companion and I, burdened as we were with an oil-burning heap, left the metal clunker in an angled parking stall on the main street of that innocent little town.

I have not knowingly littered since. And that's the thing about litter when you get right down to it. If you've littered, you know it. Admitting it may be a huge hurdle, but litterers know. And maybe the name is part of the problem. It certainly doesn't seem to be part of the solution. Why litter? Why not call it 'bigger?' Or "bitter?" The word 'litter' is misleading. It conjures up cute little animals nuzzling their momma, not unwanted waste.

But changing the name would likely achieve little. As with most character flaws, change occurs primarily through enlightenment or some life-altering personal epiphany. Perhaps that's just a bit too much to expect from your casual, everyday, garden variety litterbug.

I should note that there is some disagreement on the origin of the term 'litterbug'. Annette H. Richards claims to have created the term in 1952 when she was writing an article on vandalism in USA National Parks. As the conflict regarding the origin of the term "litterbug" is essentially between a city dweller and a country maven, this only serves to underscore the rivalry that may exists between city and country litterbugs, those poor souls who seem constitutionally incapable of controlling their personal rubbish removal behavior.

Before WW 2, in that simpler time many of us long to return to, people used most everything they owned. They had little to discard. But if they did, they likely let it drop by the wayside like an idle thought. And the times did not allow for many idle thoughts.

Book Angst - A Tale

"I believe that today more than ever a book should be sought after, even if it only has one great page in it. We must search for fragments, splinters, toenails, anything that has ore in it. Anything that is capable of resuscitating the body and the soul." ~ **Henry Miller**

I'm relatively new to Denman Island. I love this place, the quiet, the sight and the sweep of the sea. But I have some city ways that I have brought with me that seem destined to trip me up for a time. For example, I still get 'wound up.' I literally vibrate over certain issues. Revelations about the wayward meanderings of federal tax dollars just steams me. Provincial Government heartlessness and obfuscation over such issues as homelessness and the social safety net sometimes boils me over. The privatization of the highway-ferry system has nearly made me apoplectic. My significant other, who has been living here a bit longer than I, often advises me to chill out, get a grip and acclimatize slowly. "Get grounded, you big lug," she says. Good advice, I figure. And she knows I will always listen to her sage advice.

So what is one of the first things I do to gently and innocuously insinuate myself into the collective heartbeat of Denman Island? I attend the January 2004 DIRA meeting *(I have been to a few other Resident's Association meetings since first stumbling on to Denman a couple of years ago and I am pretty sure my membership fee is paid up)* and become seemingly complicit in the death of democracy. I confess, being still, in spirit, a city guy, it was I who seconded the motion to put Denman on 'the list' to maybe, someday, possibly, get a public library annex. While being on 'the list' still doesn't seem to me to be a big deal, I expect that others will be more than willing to show me the errors of my big-city thinking ways. And I will welcome any advice offered.

I love libraries. On the Lower Mainland, they proliferate. They promote literacy and community and the arts. Heck, even though we support them through our taxes, I always have this feeling when I go to the public library that I am about to get something for free. Silly feeling, but there you go. Then, in my more affluent days, I always enjoyed paying overdue fines. It seemed like I was giving something back.

But this small personal aperitif is not about the democratic process, nor is it about the virtues of the public library system. No, it is simply about the effect of the author Henry Miller on my life and a small adventure that befell me. ***caution alert***. If I stray into sensitive or delicate areas with my trifling *bon mot,* please forgive me.

In my early teens, my cousin Bob introduced me to Henry Miller's 'Tropic of Cancer.' At the time, this was forbidden and profane territory. I knew it going in. I had already explored Daniel Defoe's 'Moll Flanders,' which somehow had found a spot on the shelf of the library at Nanaimo Senior Secondary School. Miller was a different kettle of fish from Defoe. For one thing, although I was oblivious to it then, he was still alive. At the time, I believed most authors were dead. As you can see, I was worldly beyond my years. Anyways, Miller was clearly a naughty man. He swore and used all sorts of exotic language to describe how men and women interact. *(Interact is my pale euphemism for things I'd best not elaborate on.)* He wrote of mysterious doings in a faraway Paris that simply had no counterpart in my small world. To this day, it may be that I am trying to shake off the effects of that encounter with Miller, the rapscallion and dangerous author. Under the back porch of my Cousin Bob's house in East Vancouver, in the summer of 1961, I caught a glimpse of a strange sexual world. I have to say it was a salient moment in my life.

Flash forward to January, 2004. I have become a frequent user of the Dora Drinkwater Volunteer Library. One day, while scanning the eclectic biography section, I found 'Henry Miller, A Life' by Robert Ferguson. A couple of days earlier, while channel surfing, I chanced upon an old interview with Miller. With this colliding co-incidence, I took the book out. A week later, during a big snow storm, I settled in to what I hoped would be a good winter read. Page after page led me down the course of Miller's life. I was really enjoying the book. About sixty pages in, I took a breather. Now, it may help to know that one of my less desirable reading habits is that I like to thumb ahead when I am reading a book that stands a chance of being illustrated. I am a very visual person and biographies usually have at least a couple of photo sections. I innocently scrolled ahead and screeched to a halt at page 174. There, splayed between the pages, was not some pressed leaf keepsake. No? No! Some previous lover of biographies had clearly allowed his ardour to wander whilst marginally engaged in reading. There, squashed between the pages, was the clearly used prophylactic evidence, not only of a past outbreak of safe sex, but of a callous disregard for library property. The juices of his less then literate outburst had seeped through a number of the pages of this tragically despoiled book. My winter read was spent for the moment.

I gathered my strength. Soon, I was seeking written winter comfort elsewhere. However, being new to the rhythm of the rural heartbeat, my pitiful urban self simply could not unwind. The book was not mine. I needed to return it to the Dora Drinkwater. I could not simply shove it through the night deposit receptacle with no explanation of its rubbery residue. And even if I did, shouldn't I sheath the abused volume in some protective cloak? Should I include a note strongly advising that the book be purged of its soiling material? How would they do that? And who would be assigned the task? A public health nurse, perhaps? Or the Center for Disease Control? Shrapnel of weak thought overwhelmed me. Was this really my problem, for gosh sakes? I was but collateral damage, a guiltless library patron. Could anyone be more innocent then that?

Panic subsided after a time. Courage prevailed. I returned the plastic bag-encased victim of one man's *(I presume it was one man)* excesses one gloomy afternoon.

In as delicate a phrasing as possible, I described to the library volunteer who had the misfortune to be working her shift that day the horror which had befallen me, my long affection for Miller and my regret at the entire series of misadventures that had led up to this awkward moment. Relatively new to the position, she handled the bedeviling information I was imparting with a cool and amused professionalism. I completed the sorry tale, gathered a few more tomes *(none involving Miller in the slightest)* to read, giving them all the benefit of the doubt by not inspecting them for obvious signs of contamination, and departed.

You might think that, after such a disturbing encounter, I would swear off volunteer libraries and other such dangerous small town excesses. I have to believe that the desecration was some sort of accident. Any alternative scenario is too unpleasant to consider.

Having now had some time to recover, and reflect, I know I will return one day to the occasional pleasures that Miller's works afford me. Still, it will *never* be the same. This incident has also impacted how I relate to all manner of itinerant reading materials. I am finding myself resistant to magazines in Dentist and Doctors' offices and the like. When I enter *any* library now, I bide my time. I stroll hesitantly down the aisles, unable to commit. I haven't yet resorted to the wearing of plastic gloves, the kind they wear at crime scenes. The tactile pleasure found in the actual clutching and caressing of a book, as opposed to the supremely sterile experience of an internet read, hopefully will not be forever lost to me.

Breakfast Love

"He smiled rather too much. He smiled at breakfast, you know." ~ **Charles Wheeler remembering the spy, George Blake.**

Some time ago, after the exhilarating experience the previous evening of singing in the Denman Island Peace Choir, I celebrated in the way I have invariably marked significant events in my life: I went out for breakfast. I went to the Cafe on the Rock, and had a superb morning meal. The hash fries were crisp and tasty, the veggie links a rare restaurant treat, the toast thick-sliced and buttery hot, and the eggs bordered on being a miracle of precision cooking, medium hard, hinting of yoke about to run but holding fast.

As always, there in my morning element, I found the sort of tranquility mystics spend a lifetime in search of.

Breakfast has always been my meal. As a child, often the only means to get me out of bed in the morning was the promise of the morning's first feast. Alas, as time wore on, my remaining formative years were occupied with more typical youthful pursuits and breakfast became simply a source of fuel rather than the passion it once had been.

In my early twenties, I travelled east in search of meaning and an enlightenment that was eluding me. After many days on the road, I arrived in Toronto. There, I spent fall and winter freeloading with friends and poking about that great Mecca.

Toronto, in those days, was rich with morning eating emporiums. Greasy spoons littered the landscape. For the next three months, I went out every morning to a different breakfast palace. The friends I was crashing with weren't charging me rent but they had little, so I felt obligated to eat out as often as I could. I had a stash of money from labouring in the Northwest Territories and most of it was spent that winter on satiating my quest for the perfect first meal of the day.

As I recall that frenetic time, I am appalled by my own gluttony and shallowness. It is also somewhat disconcerting to think that, while man was taking giant leaps into space, I spent the end of the sixties diving daily into pools of cholesterol.

As I matured, I managed to curtail many of my breakfast excesses. I left meat in the dust and successfully struggled to find some capacity to tolerate yogurt, dry toast, fruit, unadulterated hard-boiled eggs, granola and the like. And I married.

"Oh yes, there is a vast difference between the savage and the civilized man, but it is never apparent to their wives until after breakfast." ~ **Helen Rowland, Cymbals and Kettle-drums, A Guide to Men (1922).**

If I was to identify one magnificent change marriage wrought on me, it was that it simultaneously tamed my dietary flamboyances and substituted sensible eating procedures. I doubt I could have predicted this metamorphosis from the sumptuous creativity displayed by my love the first morning we shared breakfast together. She proved to be an excellent chef and whipped up a spectacular cream cheese and anchovy omelet that was our meal for some years to come.

Time and marriage were destined to alter both of us. As close as we became, our respective approaches to that most intimate and pleasurable of marital activities, the morning meal, went in quite different directions. My love oozes patience and casualness in her morning routine. She thoughtfully rises from bed, engages the cats in some polite and loving chitchat, gathers her thoughts, and, after a time, chooses some small edible nourishment that will transition her to a higher level of serenity. I, on the other hand, barrel out of bed like a freight train roaring down the Rockies, commence a dozen kitchen tasks all frantically aimed at cleaning and clearing and cooking some absolutely essential, life-affirming food. Against a backdrop of the radio blaring, the kettle pulsating, the toaster twitching and innocent cats underfoot scurrying for safety, I am completely fixated on having my breakfast before Armageddon arrives.

Only after this frenzied morning schedule am I able to address the expectations of the day with calm and deliberation.

"My wife and I tried two or three times in the last 40 years to take breakfast together, but it was so disagreeable, we had to stop." ~ **Winston Churchill, in a letter to a friend.**

Unlike Churchill's experience, my love and I try to come together to break breakfast bread at least a few weeks each and every year. We are able to curb the excesses of our respective routines sufficiently to reach a mutual morning synchronization. I take a deep breath and slow my pace; she treats me like a big pussycat; the cats venture out in recognition that breakfast harmony is afoot. For that brief time, the morning is as still as a glass of water and we all glow with breakfast love.

A Popular Culture Ode

"Most of the old time residents see gentrification as a threat; the gangs see fresh meat." ~ **Attending police officer at the scene of a shooting of a wine boutique owner in CSI NY, March 2nd, 2005.**

Early March was the first time I twigged that the word gentrification has wriggled its way into popular television. You'll excuse me if I have missed its presence in earlier productions. In any case, in this episode of *CSI NY,* three gang-bangers shoot the owner of a wine boutique. The first response cop/social commentator offers the above explanation for the shooting. He posits that the gangs can accept the gentry into their midst because the newcomers provide new victims-fresh meat as it were. Later on, we discover that this particular character is the father of one of these gang-bangers, the youth being the by-product of one of those casual infiltrations that typically set the stage for full-scale gentrification. The script falls off the gentrification rails at this point and fails to provide a serious examination of the conditions that breed gangs, other than the reference to how the one offspring of the cop-social commentator came to be bred. And I'm sure you know that story: dedicated cop, married to the job, with a spouse at home tending the hearth, saves the local girl from some awful inner-city quirky attack and then is rewarded with some hanky-panky plot development.

But, as I started to think about gentrification as plot device, I began to sense that it had been there all the time, a deep recurring, repetitive theme of change, strangers in our midst, east versus west, north at odds with the south, the frontier on the move. This was made crystal clear a few days later when I had the opportunity to watch an episode of *Have Gun Will Travel*. Did I happen to mention that I am a sucker for old westerns? Well, I am.

My first television viewing experience occurred down the street from my family's home on Seventh Street in Nanaimo in the early 1950's. My first television show *(and imagine, if you will, how wistful I am as I struggle to uncover these mysterious memories)* was either a western, *The Range Rider,* or, God forbid, a questionable, probably racist sit-com named *Amos and Andy*. As a revisionist, you can appreciate that I prefer to lay claim to *Range Rider* as my first.

Television in the fifties and the early part of the sixties was rife with western fare. The crème de la crème for me was *Have Gun Will Travel*. Paladin, Richard Boone's black-draped, literate, Mr. Fancy Pants was a complete character, full-bodied and sophisticated. He lived in San Francisco, in the Carlton Hotel of all places, attended the opera, wined and dined an amazing array of women, kibitzed alternately with 'Hey Boy' and 'Hey Girl,' *(two delightful 'menials' in the hotel's employ)* who seemed at the beck and call of Mr. Paladin, and who were treated almost as equals. Paladin lived a rich life and earned his way by contracting out his skill at weapons, diplomacy, mediation and violence to small town America.

In that early March episode, entitled *The Bostonian,* * Paladin is passing through a small Nevada town when he interrupts a local ruffian who is harassing another man by dumping his food on the ground and pushing him about. A pack of locals' cheer on this brutish behavior. The harassed man is a displaced, high-toned easterner, a remittance man of sorts, who has been exiled to the west because he had the gall to marry a theatrical strumpet, an actress one notch up from the gutter *(at least in the eyes of the easterner's blueblood relatives.)*

Paladin subsequently learns that this easterner has purchased a ranch at twice its worth, thus engendering the wrath of the local citizenry, especially a landowner who coveted the property. Further on in the episode, Paladin assists the easterner to appreciate that his purchase of the land at an excessive price gave the citizenry good cause to resent him. *They* were the true pioneers; *they* had tamed the land; *they* had spilled blood, sweat and more than their fair share of tears in the creation of their mythical west, and *he* needed to appreciate their hardship, their sacrifice.

With this Palladian observation to chew on, the easterner begins to have an epiphany. He seems to accept that his decision to pay an exorbitant amount for the land that he wanted has upset the natural order. He briefly walks a few footsteps in the boots of those he is trying to live amongst. He recognizes that right and wrong is not a simple concept and he cannot simply assume that his position is the correct one. Sadly, this insight seems to diminish when he and Paladin explore ways in which the easterner can get employees to man his cattle ranch. They determine that the only way he can survive his ranching enterprise is to pay higher wages than his enemy, the local rancher he out-maneuvered. While this pretty much chucks the intrinsic worth of his recent epiphanic enlightenment, it's a reasonable action for him to take. This of course irritates the local guy and he goes off the deep end. All of his hands jump ship and go to work for the easterner who is paying the higher rate. Paladin catches the stage to his next assignment content that he has brought the sweet as well as the sour lessons of gentrification to this small part of the Old West. Before he departs, he drops the gem that he is the president of the San Francisco Stock Exchange Club, thus emphasizing, that if there ever were any doubts about this rough and tumble gunslinger and mediator being well equipped to teach the responsibilities of gentrification to his peers, they were now invalidated.

It is clear to me, though what value it possesses is likely open to debate, that some of the essence of gentrification is to be found in celluloid tableaus like this one.

The West has been painted in film for over one hundred years. Often the heart, the predominant theme of the western movie, has been the pace of change; first nations people, pushed to the precipice of extinction; open range, claimed by cattle-owning visionaries who in turn are under assault by farmers and sheepherders and other fence-loving interlopers; the proliferation of barbed wire as a real threat to wide open grazing land as well as a metaphor for the intrusion of laws and other encroachments of unrelenting civilization; the end of the gunfighter *(brilliantly depicted in The Wild Bunch, I might add.)*

Whatever the agent of change, the old ways are constantly being pushed further west. The historian, Frederick Jackson Turner, provided a thesis in the 1890's about the loss of the American frontier and its effect on the values that Americans, up to then, had held dear. Essentially he posited that the diminishing frontier(s) had forced Americans to accept their limitations, to accept that they were an individualistic, breast-beating, patriotic, fair-playing, mobile citizenry. He argued that these qualities, coupled with the expansion and subsequent restriction of the frontier, served to define the character of its people. While Turner's peers may have had difficulty accepting his premise, Americans in general, if they were aware of his ideas, likely would have embraced them.

It may be a stretch to try to merge a notion about the loss of frontier, whether actual or celluloid, with the popular overuse of the term, gentrification. However, I would like to propose that their paths do cross on occasion. Further, these intersecting paths do suggest to me some minor universal truths about the nature of television programming, the inevitable change in the urban and rural landscape, and, most importantly, life lessons that can be learned from watching vintage oaters and current, slightly surreal, organ-dissection cop shows. Those lessons are: There is a reason beyond nostalgia why many old westerns, from the era of television and before, surface from time to time like ghostly U-boats launching waterlogged torpedoes of thought from an earlier time.

There has to be a reason why *Quincy* has spawned an army of body-dissecting versions of cop pathology. There just *has* to be.

One day, dead historians (sic) will theorize on our current preoccupation with the rampant acceleration of concerns about gentrification and maybe connect it to the world's unfettered population growth and the need for people to seek space beyond their own restrictive personal frontiers. Like, yeah!

Retro television viewing is crammed with nuggets of philosophical bon-bons well worth consuming. And finally, it is all too clear that I watch entirely too much television.

One of the three writers credited with this prophetic and insightful story was Bernie Gould who eventually went on to be one of the staff writers for the great Monty Hall game show, Let's Make a Deal

Jay's Odyssey

"He's not crazy, he's not dangerous. He's just an Island guy and sometimes you do what you need to do." ~ **Terry Glavin- writer and Island guy.**

"I'm sure we'd consider how Mr. Leggit could earn his way back aboard the ferries at some time." ~ **Almost an exact quote from Deborah Marshall, BC Ferries Spokeswoman.**

It blew onto the pages of the erratic print press like a wild and wonky Qualicum wind. Front page headlines, you'd think! Deserved to be on the front page, I figure. But I understand why the press, particularly the excessively cautious Vancouver Sun, would want to bury this intoxicatingly provocative portrait of the repercussions of the dreaded 'ferry fever syndrome' on page nine of section B of the August 6th 2005 edition of that venerable publication. After SARS and its impact on Toronto, well, let's just agree that we don't need that kind of economic panic infecting the west coast.

No denying they reported it though. The headline read *"Man who jumped from ferry in Active Pass is in trouble again."* Almost as alluring was the sub heading *(what do they call that, Walt?)* which read *"BANNED- Jay Leggit was allegedly intoxicated when he attempted to board ferry."*

The facts, as reported in the Sun, are that on the evening of July 27th last, Jay Leggit, a working man from Mayne Island, missed the ferry home. As a former part-time resident of Mayne Island, I can assure you that if you miss the ferry, there won't be another for quite some time. Mayne is sort of like the Skylab of the Gulf Islands. Well, actually, there's a whole nest of them that you had better not miss the ferry to or you're just *(can I say this?)* 'ship out of luck.'

Jay had but two choices that July evening. He could wait for the next ferry, almost guaranteed to set sail in the morning, or he could hop on the Spirit of British Columbia *(that is, a ship of the BC Ferries fleet and not just a state of west coast nirvana,)* sail part way to Active Pass, climb over those railings they put up there to kind of inhibit those who might get overwhelmed by the beauty of the Gulf Islands, *(this allure is one symptom of ferry fever syndrome,)* lean a bit too far over, and *kerplunk.* Apparently not a patient man *(though one has to wonder about that as his ostensible reason for wanting to get home that night was to play baseball with his team,)* he chose the latter option. I have to say here that any notion that Mayne Island baseball is a slow-moving, lackadaisical sort of game can be put to rest by Jay's exuberance to play baseball, *(a game of inches and fraught with oodles of down time, demanding that its participants exhibit a wealth of patience waiting for something to maybe happen.)* Plainly, there is a heightened sense of team spirit on Mayne Island that even the BC Ferries Bosses and Swabs baseball league must be compelled to admire.

Still, Jay *took* the plunge, accompanied by 'a couple of garbage bags containing personal possessions,' and hit the water a runnin'. You might quibble with his choice of personal flotation devices but you have to admire his aquatic agility. I'm trying to imagine plunging off that swift moving spirit vessel with TWO GARBAGE BAGS OF STUFF. Into Active Pass, no less; always a churning vibrating cauldron of devil's water.

So, here's Jay, bobbing in the osterized water. Ferry officials are frantic. Presumably someone noticed Jay's high dive and raised the alarm. Whether Jay hollered GERONIMO *(or some suitably Canadian lotus land holler)* as he leapt into the dark blue void, is unknown. As he plummeted down to meet his watery fate, was he recalling his last, and only, bungee jump? Was his mind expecting his body to spring back and halt his impetuous descent? Most likely Jay was totally focused on the Island, the ballgame and his teammates.

Ferry officials acted appropriately. The Spirit of British Columbia slammed on the brakes. Two other members of the fleet halted as well. Three rescue boats were launched. They found no trace of Jay though one might speculate that they may have caught a glimpse of him dragging his soggy self ashore at the old lighthouse at Helen Point.

While it is not reported if Jay made it to shore with both of his personal flotation devices intact, we do know that **"he was later arrested by Outer Gulf Islands RCMP while walking on an island road."** The report does not say whether this was before or after the ball game which, you would agree, is a valuable tidbit to which the public should be privy.

Now, apparently the singular act of taking a header *(or footer)* from a ferry is not against the law. However, the law's a tricky son of a gun. While ten lords a leaping off of a ferry is copasetic, the aggravation and trouble such a liberating and theatrical act might cause the ferry corporation and your fellow travelers may contravene some stickler's version of the rules the courts uphold. Charges are still being considered **"as a deterrent."** You smile. I understand. Most of us, I reckon, don't need Jay to be charged to deter us from such a rash performance. However, there must be something in the drinking water of Island guys because Island writer guy Terry Glavin suggests that there is a testosterone induced Island logic to catapulting off a ferry that has the temerity to not dock at your Island. It is the call of the Island sportsman, the siren call that pierces the heart of the delayed traveler, calling him home, beckoning sweetly from the supple swells of the sea, the curve of the shoreline. Unfortunately, BC Ferries, a bottom-line unimaginative corporation, simply can't fathom this urge.

Double jeopardy may have reared its hydra head in this affair. Not only is Jay possibly going to face deterrence charges, the ferry corporation has banned him. This, and his alleged euphoric state, led to his subsequent arrest at Swartz Bay ten days after his joyous leap off the liner. After his Active Pass baptism, Jay managed to escape, Napoleon-like, from his Elba. He then tried to walk on the ferry to get back home. He may have had a little too much to drink. This is understandable. Banned by BC Ferries, treated like a pariah for doing a Gertrude Bell imitation, his mind, murky from ferry fever, it is likely that he came to believe that the ferry was his way home, his I-5, his Trans-Canada.

The Corporation's heavy-handed approach to transportation and recreational sport indiscretions are worrisome. The warning signs of ferry fever syndrome are all over this case. For instance, one major component of ferry fever is the failure of the ferry corporation to accept that it is part of the highway system. This denial may be at the heart of the Corporation's image problems.

This question will not go away: should those afflicted by ferry fever be constrained from going home? If it is true that Jay was under the weather, no matter the cause, might not BC Ferries have provided some form of secure accommodation, some sea-going hoosegow, where inebriated and otherwise incapacitated passengers might cool their jets in transit? If another nautically obsessing Jay showed up at their ticket booth demanding a ride home, well, rather than bothering the RCMP who clearly are more occupied these days doing contract work for the DEA, could not Ferry officials play ball, as it were, and gently put on a combination life preserver/straight jacket on the individual in question and escort him to his travel cubicle? Sooner than you can say Jay's your uncle, he'd be home, none the worse for wear.

Ferry Fever Syndrome, or, as it has become known, Ferry Apprehensive Reactive Trauma, requires a range of responses and a sensitivity not commonly credited to large transportation monoliths. Punitive responses will not endear the BC Ferry Corporation to Islanders. And certainly, excommunication will serve no purpose other than create a cadre of martyrs to the cause of 'getting home on time to play ball' or cook supper or chop wood or really, whatever needs doing at home.

The larger issue, of course, is the battering that the Gulf islands are taking from the expectations and aspirations of the larger society. Earlier in the year, for example, Galiano Island, just a hop skip and a swim from Mayne Island, was invaded by a flotilla of Bingo Police. Having spent the previous evening reconnoitering at a luxury B & B, a battalion of gung-ho elite gambling Special Forces attacked the main Bingo Bunker on the Island and captured the sinister guru of the Island Bingo cartel in the tub. Their mission relied heavily on the complicity of the Ferry Corporation. Gambling is not allowed on board and the Corporation and its collaborators will go to any length to smite it on the Islands.

Whether it is Bingo excesses, spur-of-the-moment baseball or swimming marathons, the outer world will increasingly want to stamp out any charming island eccentricity. Couple this with the plague that is Ferry Apprehensive Reactive Trauma and the future of any peculiarity that exists on the gulf islands must be considered brittle at best.

The Birds: Film Fantasy or Nature as a Terrorist Threat?

"In the spring of 1960, a deluge of reports of dead birds reached British wildlife authorities." ~ **Rachel Carson, Silent Spring, published 1962.**

Have you ever seen Hitchcock's The Birds? I recently watched it for, oh I don't know, the umpteenth time. Some films are old friends. You don't bother keeping track of how often you meet: All that lingers after you get together is a sense of gentle familiarity and comfort. *The Birds* is one such old friend of mine.

Like many of the movies I am drawn to, *The Birds* has a poignant urban-rural tension. F'instance, we first meet Mitch Brenner and Melanie Daniels, the primary human characters in the film, deep in the heart of San Francisco. They are early sixties, hip, urban dwellers. Mitch is a criminal defense attorney, spending, as his kid sister subsequently confides, 'most of his time in jail.' He is a smooth, slick guy, perhaps an early, rough and ready version of a metrosexual. As befits the times, he is also a control freak.

Melanie, on the other hand, seems just a tad too rich for her own good; for our own good. She has a reputation, we are told, not only for playing vapid practical jokes, but for more exotic naughtiness as well; nude swimming in Italian fountains (*perhaps an urbane Hitchcockian insider tip of the hat to Fellini, the director of La Dolce Vita, released two years before The Birds*).

Mitch and Melanie are clever, bubbly people, successful and confident. Mitch is an irritatingly sharp mixture of sophisticated city chutzpah and rustic smarts. Melanie is flawed, trivial and temperamental. We recognize that she is

32

missing some down-home earthiness, (*my euphemism for whatever Hitchcock believed shallow ditsy heiresses require to get them grounded. I need to be clear here that Hitchcock was pretty much a chauvinist and manipulated his female characters, as well as the actresses he selected to play them, to emphasize their fascination with, their capacity for, foolish behavior.*) Nevertheless, an audience familiar with cinematic conceits has no doubt that Mitch and Melanie will eventually hook-up.

Hitchcock often plays sexual tension against an urban/rural landscape. In *Psycho*, for example, an impulsive act of theft, on the heels of a tawdry tryst, plummets the main character, barely thirty minutes into the movie, to a shocking, backwater death. There is a punitive morality at work here, a corrective lesson in rural revenge that catapults Marion Crane to her damp demise. Simply put the lesson is: beware those off-the-beaten-path Bed and Breakfasts, especially the ones littered with stuffed birds.

In *The Birds*, Hitchcock utilizes the good storyteller's flexibility to exploit nature as a means to test his characters, challenge them, and measure their grit.

Regrettably, rather than employ a mature means to bring his disparate twosome together, he concocts an idiotic plotline. He has Mitch's little sister (*who lives fulltime in the country*) appear to be the sort of silly child who would want a couple of caged love birds for her birthday. We are expected to swallow the notion that a country girl is so unfamiliar with wildlife that imprisoned birds are her cup of tea. Of course, Hitchcock is pulling our urban chicken legs but, nevertheless, he unites this thin thread of pablum with Melanie's inane predisposition for practical jokery. He has her purchase and transport the chirping lovey-dovey twosome to Mitch's house. She doesn't simply deliver them; she speeds across the Bay in a runabout, breaks into the house and leaves the poor flustered feathery creatures on a piece of furniture and skulks off.

"It is mankind, rather, who insists upon making it difficult for life to exist upon this planet." ` ~ Cigarette smoking, elderly ornithologist bit player in *The Birds*.

In the film, a pivotal point is reached early on, courtesy of a bloodthirsty, dive-bombing seagull and the lovely dock at Bodega Bay. Our heroine motors back to the dock after surreptitiously sneaking into her quarry's home and leaving the lovebirds (*by the way, on both a self-preservation and an animal liberation note, I believe Hitchcock was admonishing us not to buy pets as gifts. If people want pets, let them get them themselves. Nature's creatures should*

33

not be commodities. If, however, you are compelled to buy a little being and deposit it in a stranger's home that you've 'B&E'd', you may well become the deserved target of vengeful flying fowl), when a solitary seagull dive bombs her, draws blood, and flies off. Our hero rushes down the dock, intercepts our wounded heroine, and assists her to safety.

The Bodega Bay dock serves as an extension of Mitch's character, simultaneously allowing him to rush to her rescue without getting wet and emphasizing the proximity of man to water. *"Why are they doing this? They say when you got here the whole thing started."* ~ **Hysterical yet intuitive local woman berating Melanie about nasty bird behavior in *The Birds*.**

Hitchcock portrays the caged lovebirds as representative of the urban dweller's restricted spirit. He is saying that city folk who find themselves in a rural environment still seem trapped in their metaphorical cages. Oh, they can feed themselves but they only find safety within the shelter of their tiny little home. It will take them time to work free from their cubicle, learn how to survive on more than their downy cuteness.

Hitchcock's fish-out-of-water romantic plot moves at a frantic pace and in short order (*which by the way, turns out to be fried chicken at the local eatery*) nature runs amuck and the people of Bodega Bay are under winged assault by thousands of renegade feathered fiends. A sense of foreboding inhabits the film at every turn. This is commonplace in films now, the emphasis of that niggling feeling that some invasive creature or substance is poised to attack. 1950's films, particularly anti-communist and outer space invader flicks, also tapped into paranoia as art. In the early sixties, the tide was turning. There was a Doris Day sense of optimism emerging; Camelot was rising again. Hitchcock, a renowned sourpuss, wanted to curdle our puny sanguinity. *"Dive-bombing seagulls in Somerset, England, have been attacking mail postal carriers, says the Sunday Mail. One Royal Mail postie was knocked off his bike and another left sprawling in the road. For some reason, the birds have allowed women postal workers to pass."* ~ **Globe and Mail August 17 2005.**

Cinema aside, attack birds may be more prevalent than any of us care to admit. Many of us likely have a 'bird swooping down on us' tale. In the late seventies, I personally was enjoying a lunchtime stroll on a busy urban artery, when I was set upon by a deranged crow. He missed my vitals but his feathers brushed my widow's peak. I attempted to report it to the authorities but they seemed deluged with other criminal aberrations and hurried me on my way. Numbed, I foolishly put the whole crow-cussing mess down to errant gas emissions.

Not that long ago, a reliable Denman Islander expressed her fear that one day a misguided hummingbird would thrust its deadly beak into her brain and render her, well, bird-brain dead. This is not an unreasonable fear.

More common than dive-birds are bombing birds. The British Royal Mail report attests to the longevity of the concern for nature run amuck.

Recently, a thoughtful local owl allegedly took four swipes at, and a few nibbles from, a bare-headed male jogger on two separate days. Keith Wakelin summed the experience up succinctly: *"It was really freaky."*

The Birds remains a powerful cautionary tale though I suspect the army of bird lovers and watchers on Denman might not fully agree. That's cool. Still, I will maintain a modest skepticism about our feathered neighbours, especially when they gather in groups. And hang out on wires. And watch from their launching perch. The awful truth is that I simply cannot get *The Birds* out of my mind.

Hitchcock was onto something. You won't be seeing me outdoors any time soon.

Turnip Love

"A degenerate nobleman is like a turnip. There is nothing good of him but that which is underground." ~ **17th century saying.**

There are so many issues aflutter in the world today, that even I, a practitioner of tangential thought, am shocked and embarrassed that I am taking the time to ruminate on the lowly turnip. Earthquakes, hurricanes, floods, and war occupy the airwaves. I follow all of their ramifications religiously, never wavering from the belief that one has a responsibility to remain current. These events are often overwhelming; they are frequently of catastrophic size. We have witnessed the giant tsunami that steamrolled the Far East and Hurricane Katrina that sank New Orleans, not to mention the massive earthquake along the Pakistan border and the horrific death toll.

But to cope with the monumental hugeness of nature and man run ferociously amuck, I have to seek out smaller issues, tinier morsels of potentially digestible material. Hence, the story of my life and how it collided with the TURNIP. *"The candle in that great turnip has gone out."* ~ **Winston Churchill, commenting on the passing of conservative politician, Stanley Baldwin**

Growing up, my diet was a simple affair. Both of my parents had humble origins and even humbler palates. Meat and potatoes, potatoes and meat were the order of pretty much every day. These staples would often be supplemented by plain salads and boiled, sopping wet vegetables. My father, manly in ways I would never be, rarely cooked, and my mother resisted kitchen captivity except when domestically unavoidable. While I never thought of her as a stellar cook, she could whip up a fried or boiled dinner with the aplomb of a third world street vendor.

Even under these adverse conditions, my appetite was not intimidated. I was not a finicky eater. While I may not have wanted to chow down with others as regularly as my family expected, displaying an early antisocial bent I am still troubled by, once I settled in at my eating stall, I rarely left any food on the plate. That really was the key dining rule in our home: *"Finish your plate before you leave the table, Willy,"* was a frequent refrain from my pop. Food was not to be wasted.

Often, I would shovel my food down and be ready to leave the table before my mother even had a chance to join us. Clearly, I was a rude little bugger, an observation my father would frequently make. He would say, *"You're a rude little bugger, isn't he Marion?"* And my mother would say, *"Isn't he what, Sterling?"* And he would answer, *"Isn't he a rude little bugger? He doesn't even have the decency to wait until you sit down."* And she would refrain, *"Let the boy eat, Sterling. Can't you see he's hungry?"*

By the time my father had made his initial observation, he was half way through his first helping. He was a hefty man, setting an unavoidable standard for me, I'm afraid. He demonstrated his love for my mother, amongst other ways, by courageously seeking out seconds of her cooking at every turn. No matter what she prepared, he christened it *"delicious, darling."* My mother would invariably look at him in adoration, turn back to what was occupying her on the stove and parry his praise with *"You're a fibber, you are. A woman can't believe a word you say. You'd eat an old leather shoe if I cooked it just right."* She knew my father's love was, in part, measured by food consumption and the absolute pleasure he found in eating.

I didn't really know it then, but my mother found equal pleasure in simply having enough to cook. Having enough was such a joy for her. Growing up, there was often little or nothing to eat, except what the surrounding countryside and family garden could provide. She was raised on a small scrub farm in the shadow of the Rockies. Her parents were the children of farmers and grew what their ancestors grew, root vegetables. Parsnips and turnips headed the list. My mother was raised on a diet of rogue weed vegetables, heavily supplemented by roots. This Spartan lifestyle strongly influenced her culinary routine. *"Ever*

since I was a wee thing, no higher than a root vegetable, I have hated turnips." ~
Bill Engleson, pretty much any time anyone cared to know.

Entering my pre-school years, I began to feel my spoiled-child oats by expressing modest likes and dislikes about food. For instance, a couple of my favorite foods were canned Chili Con Carne and Chef Boyardee Ravioli. I especially liked to eat them for breakfast. As the family's financial status improved, my mother, for reasons we never really talked about, acceded to my idiotic breakfast requests. Now, as a middling vegetarian with an occasional fish fetish, I marvel at my childhood's diet. Still, as I have noted, my mother found pleasure in seeing her children and husband eat. She found joy in providing the food no matter that it was fried, boiled beyond recognition, or scooped out of a can.

I have always refused to eat turnips. When my mother cooked them, she would leave lumps of hard pieces, barely boiled or baked hunks of root, mixed in with a stew of soggy mushy turnip shreds. Even with salt, pepper and butter, they struck an off-chord with me. On those occasions, I would lay my eating utensils down, put on my patented turnip face, the one suggesting imminent death from poisoning, and refuse to eat. If I came nose-to-nose with that agonizingly distorted face on that horrid little boy today, I would strenuously avoid recognizing his sappy ploy, purist that I am. My father, however, was of the jump- in-with-both-feet-before-you-know-how-deep-the-pond-is school of parenting. In short order, he would erupt in drill-sergeant fashion and fire a command. *"Fine, go to your room, Willy. You can eat them later."* Though the threat was always made by my father, my mother was always expected to carry out the execution. She never did. My father likely knew she never would. As the night faded, the turnip wars would lessen. My mother clearly knew that uneaten turnips were best fed to the hogs. Hog-less city dwellers that we were, she would eventually turf them into the waiting garbage can, a suitable repository, to my mind, for the troublesome turnip. *"I was the fattest baby in Clark County, Arkansas. They put me in the newspaper. It was like the prize turnip."* ~ **Billy Bob Thornton.**

As I grew older, we had turnips less and less. When we had them, the expectation that I eat the sinewy mess considerably diminished. Eventually they disappeared from my mother's modest repertoire.

On one occasion before that happened, I created a small, emotionally wrenching faux pas, when, upon returning from a church potluck, I commented positively on one of the dishes, a turnip casserole, heavily sweetened, no doubt. My mother was shattered. She tried for years to prepare the root vegetable to my liking; it had never happened. She always failed to adjust my snooty little opinion. Now, some strange woman *(I assume a church lady because it was not my experience that church men prepared potluck dishes)* had won me over. Some stranger was my turnip love.

Till the end of her days my betrayal and her failure were the source of an inordinately vast amount of mother/son banter. I came to believe that any opinion I held had less validity in the eyes of my mother. I had wavered in my opinion of the lowly turnip. She did not openly humiliate me but the sweet snicker in her voice left no doubt that one complementary slip had driven a wedge between us. *"In 1960, Denman farmers grew 318 tonnes of turnips."* ~ **Marcus Isbister-quoted in Islands in Trust, 1988.**

Today, to my surprise, I find myself living on an Island well known for turnip production. The irony has not escaped me. Recently, after a kind neighbor threatened to create a turnip dish only the most taste bud challenged could not enjoy, my love took up the challenge herself. She bought a locally grown turnip, sliced it up, steamed it and fried the slices in bread crumbs, oyster-like. I love oysters in such an inverse ratio to my feeling for the turnip that I suppose she thought a similar preparation might win me over.

Thus, for me, the worse in "for better or worse" may have come down to one later-in-marriage turnip meal. Part of me wants to abandon my childish, lifelong rejection of the aggravating turnip. What holds me back from this display of maturity is the uncomfortable sense that, if I do embrace the damn vegetable this late in life, it will have been the gravest betrayal of my mother. In this regard, my past holds me captive.

Mom may have enjoyed some of my discomfort. *"The candle in that great turnip has gone out."* ~ **Winston Churchill, commenting on the passing of conservative politician, Stanley Baldwin.**

The Beaver, Water, and Other Things on My Brain

"Alberta is the first province to permit the buying and selling of water rights. But wary aqua–nationalists, fearing a rapacious America, have bitterly resisted wider consideration of commerce in water." **Melting Point, by Chris Wood, the Walrus Magazine, October 2005.**

On a mid-May morning some time back, after a glorious week of warm, life-sustaining sun, the heavens cracked open and the rains came. Trapped with my own miscellaneous thoughts, anchored against a backdrop of Kyoto bashing by Stephen Harpoon and his gaggle of henchfolk, I forced myself to speculate about what part of the environment none of us can do without. Though air was almost at the top of my list, water won by a drip.

A few days earlier, I had seen a news report on the opening of a massive hydro-electric dam in China, a project so colossal that one million people were to be permanently dislocated. If anything underscores the length government will stretch itself to achieve more power, hydroelectric or political, China's rush to devastate the lives of such fantastic numbers of its people provides a cataclysmic emphasis.

Lucky sot that I am, I've never had to give access to water much thought. However, for about twenty years before migrating to Denman Island, we owned rural property on Mayne Island and belonged to the Georgina Water Works. It was only then that I finally understood what that Monopoly card meant. Nevertheless, water really was nothing more than a commodity to conserve. If we'd stayed on Mayne, we would have participated in the consolidation of the various waterworks which now compose a network on that island, an island dependent on groundwater as its primary source. Check it out at www.mayneislandchamber.ca/water.html *"Once, during Prohibition, I was forced to live for days on nothing but food and water."* ~ **W.C. Fields.**

World Water Day came and went that year on March 22nd without so much as a mention by anyone I spoke to that day. There it sat, smack dab in between my birthday, seven days earlier, and my love's birth anniversary, seven days after. And we missed it.

A few weeks later, almost completely recovered from Stephen's election and enjoying the irony of a reform government going to ground to escape scrutiny, I caught an episode of **'Leave it to Beaver'** that smacked of true tinsel-town prophesy:

The Stage; High Summer. Everyone's sweating, like in a scene from any Tennessee Williams play. The youth of the neighbourhood, in need of cash to buy baseball uniforms, are labouring away cutting lawns, trimming hedges and the like. The nickels and dimes are rolling in.

Excluded from these typical teen cash-raising activities because he's still a little squirt, Theodore Cleaver (*the Beaver*) is out and about, killing time. City workers let slip that they will be turning the water off for a few hours to fix a water main leak. With this small pool of insider knowledge, Beaver, with the instincts of a Donald Trump, decides a water shortage might just prove a windfall for him. *"Thousands have lived without love, not one without water."* ~ **W.H. Auden**

Beaver fills as many containers as he can with tap water and starts circulating around the neighborhood. Pretty quickly, the whole community is aware that the water has been shut off. He has a small monopoly. Word spreads that he's the go-to guy for the precious aqua. His friends and their families are forced to fork out most of their loose change for Beaver's water. *(Sounds a tad brackish, doesn't it?)*

Beaver prospers. He has cornered the market. His peers, however, find his profiteering repellant. They grouse that they would never do what Beaver has done. They call him a crook.

"Why it might lead to juvenile delinquency...or communism" **Tooey's mom, in reference to Beaver selling water.** Water, as a commodity, rightly concerns Tooey's mother. *(Tooey is one of the Wally Cleavers buddies.)* In her

simulated 1950's kitchen, she opines that if only one entity controls the distribution of a necessary item *(in this case one smart pintsize cookie, Beaver Cleaver, who has a brief lock on the water market)*, then this is communism. She doesn't like this red specter. More than her disgust at the Beav's fellow traveler inclinations, she doesn't like not having access to water.

How could this dilemma not strike a chord with Americans of the day? And is it that much different today? Canada continues to be seen as a communist stronghold by a sizable chunk of Americans, second only in the hemisphere to Cuba. The undeniable fact *(though some argue fiction)* that we have a lot of water must rankle then to no end. *"Whiskey is for drinkin'; water is for fightin'."* ~ **Attributed to Mark Twain (1835-1910).**

The episode ends on an especially optimistic, gloriously entrepreneurial note. Beaver learns that the water shortage will lead to a '*lectricity*' outage overnight and shares this nugget with his older peer tormentors. They decide to corner the candle market and make a killing. The moral, I suppose, is that everyone is out to make a buck in America. And can, if you create shortages. Like water. Like land even. *The wars of the twenty-first century will be fought over water."* ~ **Ismail Serageldin, World Bank V.P. for Environmental Affairs quoted in "Water" by Marq de Villiers 2000.**

As we examine our OCP *(Official Community Plan)* and tweak it inexpensively, I cannot help but join my voice with those who see water as the pivotal factor in the future of our Island. The outer world understands the worth of water. High end water is being sold in the world's boutiques at extraordinarily disproportionate prices. By contrast, some islanders here have no natural source and are forced to buy in bulk. It is not hard to envision mercenaries escorting shipments of cool clear water to all of the earth's dry and drier places. It is not hard to imagine a slightly smarter U.S. of A. President *(it's really not hard to imagine that)* sending troops to Canada to get whatever water that big, thirsty, sweaty country wants.

Talk about wet dreams! *"I overheard not too long after moving here about an attempt fifty years ago to pipe mountain water from the Beaufort Hills to Denman Island. It would have cost $300 per family, a monumental sum in those days. The plan was rejected. I have to think that the fear of an imminent water shortage was on the minds of Denman Islanders a long time ago. What did they* *know then that we might want to consider?" ~ Rural Roberts, (a pen name of mine. And yes, I am quoting my alter ego.)*

Our OCP goes to some length to ban the piping in of water from elsewhere. I suppose this makes sense. Americans, on the other hand, seem poised to build a new dam, just south of us. Nothing holds them back. If they do build this dam, one possible repercussion might be significant flooding in Canada, a backwash of America's lust for water power.

When I started to write this cogitation, I wanted nothing more than to talk about my spurious thesis that TV shows from the 1950's might have something to teach us today. In hindsight, *(where I have my best vision located)* this is such a ludicrous proposition that I have wandered off into a more solemn subject. *"Currently the Trust is seeking to have the Ministry of the Environment undertake a ground-water study on Denman and Hornby." Denman Islander, pg. 7 November 30 1990 edition.*

Water shortages. Water studies. Time bounces back like a bad penny. Here I sit in the shank of the year, wondering about the water streaming below me, wondering if anyone knows where it begins and where it wanders.

At heart though, I am not a serious person; and all this thinking has made me thirsty.

Rural Short Hairs

"In shorts, all good things are wild and free(zing)" ~ **Denman Island propaganda**

As you climb the steep hill of Denman Road up to the bluff, a plywood message wall opposite Pickles Road greets you. For a time, the above quote occupied one of the panels. At one point some wag added the *zing*-er at the tail end of the quote.

This philosophical observation got me to thinking one day. I am a man drawn to the wearing of short pants. When people who know me think of me, they likely observe in no special order, 'he's tall', 'he's bald', or 'he wears shorts'. For as long as I can remember, an ever diminishing span of time I hasten to add, I have worn shorts. I love the feel of drafty air on my legs. I relish the liberation that befalls me when my pins are uncovered. In winter, I yearn for that cold pressed seasonal chill that snaps my knees to attention. The more my legs endure the elements the warmer the rest of me seems to be.

Summer sees millions of short-panted men and women all around the world. The range of shorts available truly boggles the mind. Denim shorts, khaki, cotton, and wool *(yes, wool!)* and, I suppose, hemp shorts, are but a few of the materials that make up the world of tiny pants. And the colours. Well, an infinitesimal pallet of hues has added a broad sweep of choice in shorts as well as every other consumer product imaginable.

On charming little Denman Island, people often begin chatting with me about the shorts I appear to habitually be in. If I have chosen to drape myself in long pants, or a skirt *(okay, I don't typically wear skirts but in my youth, I was known to cross-dress while camping)* they invariably comment on the change. As a relative new comer, it seems I've staked out a certain quaint turf. So, I am biased in favour of short pants. *"A child learns to discard his ideals whereas a grown-up never wears out his short pants."* ~ **Karl Kraus (1874-1936) Austrian satirist.**

I have bought very few new clothes since my move to Denman Island. Even in my professional life, which lasted quite a bit longer then I would have hoped, my clothing budget was minimal. Smudges and faded material rarely fazed me. Then, as now, I am happiest *(and I accept that the furtherance of happiness is not typically the purview of the employer class)* when I wear shorts. In my work world this was mostly tolerated by my succession of supervisors. On occasion, looks were delivered *(in the traditional raised eyebrow way superiors have for showing their disdain)* suggesting, perhaps, that I was pushing the short pants envelope. I was, I believe, admirably able to control my bare legged excesses. For example, my labour involved some Court work. Though I often fantasized about wearing dress shorts to Court, my cowardly inner dresser simply did not have the chutzpah. *"Hain't we got all the fools on our side? And ain't that a big enough majority in any town?"* ~ **Mark Twain (1835-1910) The Adventures of Huckleberry Finn.**

As if we on Denman Island did not have enough issues to occupy our fracas engagement quota, BC Ferries has brilliantly manufactured the most nimble-witted discord imaginable. Ferry crews *(throughout the fleet so it's not like they have specifically targeted Denman)* are now banned from wearing short pants. Bare legs apparently run the risk of injury. As a caring employer, the Ferry Corporation has no choice but to protect those poor souls caught in their sticky wicket employment net from themselves, and push them firmly towards safe and proper attire. However, one aspect of Denman life seems to have evaded the nominally productive brains trust at BC Ferries Central. Though the OCP speaks about the 'social fabric' of Denman, it fails to identify an aspect of Island life that more than almost any other characteristic defines 'our Denman way'. You can pretty much dress *(or undress)* any way you like on Denman. This quirk of our character should be reflected, I would argue, in how the outer, corporate world engages us. *"... short trousers are not appropriate for any shipboard personnel. Ultimately, this is an issue of safety for our passengers and crew, fleet-wide."* ~ **Captain George Capacci, VP Fleet Operations BC Ferries in a response to an Islander.**

Upon hearing about the new policy on shorts, I wrote to Captain Capacci, the VP in charge of pants. Here is an excerpt from my letter, not yet replied to:

"I understand that a lengthy consultation occurred, in house, with a host of long-panted senior managers within BC Ferries. Thank God you were courageous enough to fly in the face of common sense for the ultimate good of us all.

I know I will feel safer from now on knowing that the crew of open deck ferries will be more alert, not to say more professional looking, as they sweat and swelter in their flame-proof polyester long pants. Often, I have heard it said that BC Ferries crew wearing short pants seem to be actually enjoying their job, seem to be promoting a positive and convivial relationship with passengers, especially tourists, in the peak, heated summer months. Clearly BC Ferries agrees with me that this sort of intimate public relations is not beneficial to the Corporation and BC Tourism in general. It promotes a rather lax and casual relationship between employees and customers of a sort not tolerated in most legitimate business endeavors."

Well, that's the long and the '*shorts*' of it. In the odd alienated world of BC Ferries, staff, though not necessarily doomed to get the '*shorts*' end of the stick, are still, somehow, '*shorts*' changed.

I'm not sure how we can support our ferry workers so that they will be treated as adults who know how to dress appropriately. One way I suppose would be the traditional nude protest. How many trips loaded with naked Islanders travelling back and forth between Denman and Buck Naked Bay would it take before BC Ferries accepted that their bunk was short sheeted? Perhaps we'll find out. Don't ask me though. I've seen myself naked. I'll be wearing my shorts.

Rural Censorship – A POV

"...censorship often boils down to some male judges getting to read a lot of dirty books - with one hand." ~ **Robin Morgan, U.S. author, feminist.**

Two years ago, *'Book Angst - A tale'* was the first article I submitted to the Flagstone. It arduously *(in 1391 words)* told the chronicle of my grimy encounter with an unabashed ejaculator's smearing of one of the Dora Drinkwater's finer biographies and my second-hand victimization by same. The sordid subject, which I attempted to present in a mildly droll fashion, was fairly unseemly stuff. I had modest misgivings about submitting it to the Flagstone, concerned perhaps that children or innocent émigrés from points beyond the Rockies might be less than amused. Being new to Denman, I had no idea what locals might find humorous, what they would be prepared to tolerate. *"Freedom of press is limited to those who own one."* ~ **H.L. Mencken**

Articles in recent editions of the Flagstone have re-stimulated me to consider the ever-queasy question of censorship; who, for example, is best positioned to censor? Is it the publication itself? The reader? The author? Most writers likely engage in some measure of self-censorship. We may not name it as such, but editing is a process of suppression, selection, in short, censorship. Choices are made constantly. Can I say this? Is this the best way to express this idea? How will this be received? Is there a better way to say it?

In a small community, the responsibility for how and what you express publicly is, I believe, much greater than it is in the outer world. The threat of a slight or insult seems so palpable in a tiny, contained society such as Denman. Those who choose to express themselves in print, or in public session, should exhibit vigilance and a concerned awareness of the potential repercussions of their words.

Beyond self-regulation, the final arbiter, in the case of printed matter, is the editor. The Flagstone appears to me to print pretty much anything that is submitted. Aside from those of us who get slagged or pigeon-holed by someone's less *(or more)* than carefully crafted contribution, this appears to be the way people want their monthly journal. The editors, of course, can clarify what their policy is on material submitted, but all the poetry and idle ramblings I have offered have seen the light of day. This suggests to me that they have an easy going and generous screening policy. *"Ideas are far more powerful than guns. We don't allow our enemies to have guns. Why should we allow them to have ideas?"* ~ **Josef Stalin.**

The question then might arise, what sort of community censorship do we have on Denman? Graffiti, for example, is both institutionalized *(The Denman Hill wall)* and anarchic *(concrete divider art)*. Somewhere in between is the plethora of bulletin boards attached to public and private buildings. Fox's Denman Commons Blog is perhaps an electronic cousin of the Flagstone and may have a similar editorial policy.

The Denman Hill wall is an ongoing and informative work of art, ideological expression, and news. It is seen to promote positive and community-minded messages. Occasionally, it falls victim to renegade thinking but, for the most part, it remains a colourful and unifying messenger of community interest.

The concrete dividers, recent additions to the 'village' streetscape, *(added, so I understand, to save lives by regulating our alleged Wild West-like parking excesses)* have brought little in the way of beauty or consensus.

Aerosol-addled scribblers scrawl their terse thoughts on the barriers from time to time. Encon dutifully paints over these hastily squirted artistic endeavors. Most of us, I reckon, thank our heavenly stars that someone, somewhere in authority is protecting us from these occasionally unsightly and awkwardly presented expectorations.

Our various community bulletin boards seem to be randomly cleansed of their overlapping clutter. Unsigned documents run the irregular risk of being purged faster than you can say D.H. Lawrence. For the most part, public announcements and personal notices stay up until the paper dries and cracks and flutters to the ground, or a thumb tack loses its grip. Time is a slow, inevitable censor. *"If liberty means anything at all, it means the right to tell people what they don't want to hear."* ~ **George Orwell.**

Perhaps one of the greatest dangers of living in a small community is the potential to only espouse safe, non-threatening epithets. The balance between suffocating complacency and nudging sacred cows is precarious. I have determined that any messages or nuggets of nuance I might want to impart are best done in a witty, sardonic way *(aside from this somber little piece that is)*. *"It is the suppression of the word that gives it the power, the violence, the viciousness."* ~ **Lenny Bruce.**

Lenny was not talking about the word 'blank.' He was talking about the word 'fuck.' He could easily have been talking about any word or idea that offended. Which I figure is pretty much any word or any idea that you can imagine.

Anyway, I think writers should offend every once in a while. We often have an irresistible impulse to stir things up. What we should never do, however, is bore. This article is 911 words, somewhat under the Flagstone's 1000 word bore quotient. If you have been bored by it, I apologize.

As you can tell, I continue to struggle with the art of self-censorship.

More *(or less)* Committee Love

"They'll nail anyone who ever scratched his ass during the National Anthem." ~ **Humphrey Bogart (1899-1957) in reference to the House Un-American Activities Committee.**

Committees should rarely engender strong emotion. Most of the zillion committees that have existed, still do exist, or will come into play down the organizational Chunnel, will go about their business with the substance of shadow, the sex drive of a eunuch. The sun will grapple mightily to illuminate them.

From time to time, a committee of substantial sway will rise like a sinister Phoenix. Such was HUAC, the House Un-American Activities Committee. Like a pack of rabid doggerel, it nipped and snarled at the soft fleshy buttocks of liberty for half a dozen years in the late forties-early fifties. It became what no committee should ever become, seriously unpleasant and full of itself.

Most committees are more palatable. Still, anytime a group forms with a desired outcome in mind, the wise among us will pay some heed to it, give some oversight, some cursory care. *"Any committee that is of the slightest use is composed of people who are too busy to want to sit on it for a second longer than they have to."* ~ **Katharine Whitehorn (b. 1926) Journalist "Are You Sitting Comfortably?" Observations 1970.**

Soliciting members to a committee can be a daunting task. For example, if you know what you want the outcome of a committee to be, you would do well to select only those people who are in accord with your goals. Though you may be tempted to select from a range of people, to give the perception that the committee is balanced and democratic, by doing so, you may well sow the seeds of failure. This possible failure of mission can be mitigated, however, especially if the committee is accountable to a larger body. Regardless of a committee's recommendation, the astute activist can always rally a membership backlash that will demand revision of the committee's recommendations, bringing them more in line with the original expected outcomes. Aside from the time spent in fomenting a planned backlash, it is likely you will have spent less time doing that than if you had participated in the committee.

Busy people generally don't have time to sit on committees. Their time is much better spent planning collective action to neutralize rogue committee missteps. *"A committee is a group that keeps minutes and loses hours"*. ~ **Milton Berle**

Some committees are known as 'ad-hoc.' Beware 'ad-hoc' endeavors. They can take on a life of their own. They sound temporary, as if they have only a brief moment to sputter. I have participated in 'ad-hoc' committees that have had the durability of Dracula. They also demand a currency similar to that extracted by the Count. Ad-hockery is a serious business. It needs to be focused, deliberate. Time is of the essence. If an ad-hoc committee hasn't identified and achieved its intent within a year, it may well become its own organization with dues paying expectations, secret ceremonies, and the ultimate insidious goal of celebrating its Centenary. *"To get something done, a committee should consist of no more than three men, two of whom are absent."* ~ **Robert Copeland.**

The most effective committee, some argue, is a committee of one. In many ways, we are all our own best committee. But, in addition to no man *(or woman)* being an Island, no man *(or woman)* should be a committee *(even on an Island)*. Yes, one person is much more efficient than two or three or more. But committees are not necessarily meant to be efficient. Rather, they often exist simply to examine an issue from every conceivable direction *(and then some.)* If they succeed in seeing the big picture, they often fossilize, having discovered that there is no truly unobjectionable answer to any dilemma. *"The state of the world would be exactly the same if I had played ping-pong instead of sitting on committees and writing books and memoranda."* ~ **Leonard Woolf.**

Some committees appear to exist in a parallel universe. Perhaps a fantasy committee might serve to illustrate. Let us suppose that we have a group of people diligently working away. Let's call the committee DUAC, the Denman United Archival Committee. It is charged with collecting the history of all the committees that have ever served Denman Island. As we know, who served on what committee and what each and every committee did or didn't do is likely to get blurred over time. Records are lost or turned to dust. Memories fade.

DUAC could serve an indispensable role. It could assemble all the documents of past doings. It would benefit generations of future Denman Island Committee members, most not yet born. It would leave a legacy of what we were talking about 'back then.' This would be a vital guidepost to what we should be talking about in the future so that there is consistency and barely noticeable change.

The reality is that all communities require a system of committees to do the work that needs doing. People like me, who poke fun at committees, do a grave disservice and I often regret my ill-thought, juvenile attempts at humour. If I had any moral fiber, I would resign from the garden of committees I have planted myself in and play more ping-pong. And, inevitably, form the Denman Island Ping Pong Players Club *(DIPPPC.)*

Book *(and other Global)* Worming Concerns

"Books are fatal: they are the curse of the human race. Nine-tenths of existing books are nonsense, and the clever books are the refutation of that nonsense. The greatest misfortune that ever befell man was the invention of printing." ~ **Benjamin Disraeli.**

Some time ago, I was at my station at the Dora Drinkwater Library. Late in the day, a woman entered. She explained that she was in the process of disposing of her late brother's possessions. He had only just moved to Denman when death claimed him. He was an erudite man and had a vast collection of books, most still in boxes. Her brother, she related, had thought highly of the Dora Drinkwater Library. Could we help her?

As she spoke, we both casually scanned the rather confined, L-shaped room that is the Dora Drinkwater Library (*the DD*). Most of the walls are completely covered with bookshelves, chock-full of reading matter. Four aisles, crammed with bound as well as unbridled volumes, reach out jetty-like from the overly engaged walls. All useable space is jam-packed. Shelves sag like cartoon sway-back horses, an image those of us prone to remember the most trivial of things might recall.

No matter the condition of some of our challenged shelves, the DD, though constricted, is sufficient for our frugal, somewhat unambitious needs. There is no extra space. Our tenancy is not dissimilar to that of a much-loved, homeless, old, vagabond uncle given a room in the basement to live out his days, thankful for shelter and comfort. *"Books for general reading always smell badly. The odor of common people hangs about them."* ~ **Nietzsche.**

I wish there was enough space in the DD for every book seeking entry. There isn't, of course, but that doesn't make the wish any less ardent. The DD is often given boxes of books by the most well-meaning people, folks adjusting their lives, managing their own cherished clutter, dutifully, inevitably downsizing. Though the re-gifted books are occasionally thematically synchronized, more usually they are a pooch's repast of written bliss.

Some reek. Some don't. As most bookworms know, books not stored with the care of fine wine acquire a moldy musk, like ripe, under-washed unwhisperables. Nonetheless, the consoling mustiness of the DD is, from time to time, enhanced by the apparition-like appearance of lovingly off-loaded, shed-stored, printed matter seeking a nook to live out their final pages. Few are turned away; many are, however, redirected for sale or some less mercenary disposition. If you have observed guilt-laden, DD librarians skulkingly depositing sacks of superfluous books at the Old School, often in the muted light of night, it is an unseemly and disquieting portrait not soon forgotten. *"Some books are to be tasted, others to be swallowed, and some few to be chewed and digested"* ~ **Bacon's Essays: Of Studies**

Recently, we were blessed with a container of cooking books. I am drawn to cooking books in much the same way that I am magnetically pulled to a well written obituary. The best of both share a skillful summary of the ingredients and an adroit synopsis.

I have collected recipes for years and, in the TBD *(Time Before Denman)*, when especially moved by the brilliance of some gastronomic word-slinger, actually made a purchase.

Alas, these dust-covered, proffered kitchen tomes, God bless 'em, were, from my perspective, trapped in a terminal time twist. Though none appeared, on a skim read, to encourage the mangled, stomach spinning medicinal benefits of jellied aspic, they still managed to harken back to a long-gone culinary era. Photos of the feasts inside seemed unappetizingly washed out like the sun-ravaged pictures of meals glued on the outer walls of worn-out, on-the-skids family restaurants, way past their prime, seeking only to prepare one final, botulism-free offering before the health inspector triggers the coup de grace. *"I have given up reading books; I find it takes my mind off myself."* ~ **Oscar Levant.**

I have struggled in my own life to pare down my personal cookbook collection. For the last few years I have relied almost totally on internet recipe websites.

Upon arriving on Denman, my love sprung a spring housekeeping directive: *"Hey, big chef, you haven't opened some of these cook books in years? Have you? 'Fess up."* And so, we trimmed my arsenal down a whit, donating a chunk of them to the free store. Oddly, one of the dispatched books, a somewhat gaudy and ill-conceived compilation of patriotic U.S. of A. recipes called, I believe, Americana Cooking *(a Christmas gift from a desperate nephew)* reappeared as a donation to the DD some weeks later. I suspect some husbandly gourmand stumbled across it in the free store's cellar book bin, momentarily imagining he might be allowed to keep it. *"The multitude of books is making us ignorant."* ~ **Voltaire.**

But, back to my real thesis; In our island homes, and in much of a world that unabashedly consumes, zillions of books and journals, laden with dust, cobwebs, and, more frequently than we might want to admit, dried dregs of home cooking, slowly and silently prepare to pounce. No one dares talk about this pending cataclysm, this voluminous volcano of parchment lava waiting to overwhelm us.

In our feeble naiveté, we continue to produce additional zillions of books *(over 60,000,000 Da Vinci Codes alone)* without a moment's thought. Unlike bottle and drinking-can manufacturers, who are obliged to charge a small stipend to encourage recycling, book publishers require no such levy. These rapacious titans continue to pour out their prodigious product, inundating us, with nary a concern for our descendants' capacity to manage this calamitous legacy. *"Well, it's a job just like any other. Good work with lots of variety: Monday, we burn Miller; Tuesday, Tolstoy; Wednesday, Walt Whitman; Friday, Faulkner; and Saturday and Sunday, Schopenhauer and Sartre. We burn them to ashes and then burn the ashes. That's our official motto."* **Guy Montag (Oscar Werner's character) in the film of Ray Bradbury's novel Fahrenheit 451.**

While things do get a little out of hand in Fahrenheit 451, I would never argue for the state-sanctioned wholesale immolation of books.

Given the gun registry debacle, and being reasonably certain that there are, quite likely, fewer guns than books in Canada, our Federal Government may not have sufficient resources to address this lollapalooza of a peril.

However, there may be no need for public policy. It may emerge that the proliferation of books is not, as I argue, an epidemic waiting to happen. It may transpire that most of us will discard a life's accumulation of books quietly, clandestinely, unaided.

On the other hand, if I am right, I would ask that you appreciate that the Dora Drinkwater is already bursting at the seams. Prune thoughtfully before you leave your bundle on the doorstep. *A few books in...a few books out*. That we can manage. In the absence of any other, *that may prove to be OUR official motto*.

Parking Lots But Enjoying Them Less

"I am leaving the town to the invaders: increasingly numerous, mediocre, dirty, badly behaved, shameless tourists." ~ **Brigitte Bardot, (On leaving her home in Saint Tropez.)**

Many would argue *(a decidedly evolved Denman skill-set)* that Denman Island is a petite piece of paradise. I'm not so effusive. I do grant that our isle shares some general characteristics most of us attribute to paradise; It's often quiet, yet not silent and it's nominally tolerant of differences without being too self-righteously sappy.

On the negative side of the ledger however, it fails glumly to absolve itself of old, lingering wounds, preferring instead to clutch the past to its ever-bruised and bruising bosom. Still, the small positives shine. The people and the natural beauty often glow. It bears little resemblance to those qualities Bardot attributed to St Tropez. And, above all else, parking is free. As I planned my doddering years, that was the deal maker.

If anything chased me from my urban enclosure, it was, in addition to the escalating roar and rage of traffic, the unrelenting cost of parking. I would go to extreme lengths to avoid feeding those gluttonous meters. As for pay parking lots, I occasionally found myself in their beckoning clutches. On the verge of ensnarement, I would go the extra distance, piloting my steed to an inconvenient, distant, no-cost/low cost side street. Not very environmentally aware, I admit, but such was the desperation I felt when about to be privately taxed for deciding, every now and then, to park my car and stop burning carbon fuels for a brief time. What finally irked me was the day my City Hall decided to charge its residents for the privilege of parking *at* the City Hall lot. To conduct business with staff and elected officials, no less. Denman doesn't have a City Hall. Yet! That too was a deal maker. *"We should declare war on North Vietnam…We could pave the whole country and put parking strips on it, and still be home by Christmas."* ~ **Ronald Reagan.**

Denman is by no means the only local area where parking meters haven't sprouted. Courtenay, Comox and Cumberland are but a few of the surrounding communities where common decency has prevailed, where taxes are taxes and parking is as much of a pleasure as it can be.

And Union Bay. You can pull off 19A and just stop. Dead in your tracks. You could probably camp in downtown if you weren't too obvious about it. And no meter maids. Or meter lads. The provisional absence of parking meters in these relatively small communities seems to me to promote a welcoming feeling, a hale and hearty 'come on in,' a sense of simplicity, of downright acceptance. By contrast, parking meters and parking lots in the city are the antithesis. They are there to aggravate the traveler, to keep people on their guard, nervous and ill at ease, reminding one and all that you only have so much time and you'd better hurry along before the tow-truck, hearse-like, comes to haul your vehicle to the bone yard.

I can't explain Tofino *(who can?)* which recently decided to extract every possible penny they could bleed from their local and tourist population by installing parking meters. I understand this initiative has suffered a setback of late which is only fair and just. *"Politics is not worrying this Country one-tenth as much as where to find a parking space."* ~ **Will Rogers (1879-1935).**

Pay parking lots and meters may or may not be in our future. However, how and where, and for that matter, why we park are very topical issues. For example, many of us wheel into flexible, slightly imaginary parking stalls up and down the commercial length threaded by Northwest Road. Most highly illegal! Very unsafe! That aside, there is a Wild West, liberating, anarchic, yet vaguely predictable quality to our parking patterns.

When I think about Downtown Denman, you know, that bucolic, slightly imaginary village of Downtown Denman, cleaved by the eminently practical Northwest Road, I think, how long can this chaotic parking autonomy continue? This gnarly subject arose in OCP discussion recently on the future of Denman Village. The sprawl-like quality of our downtown core reflects these simmering parking tribulations. *"Bakery Parking"* **five new signs planted not so long ago on a small hillock at the Bakery.**

The bakery signs appeared some time ago, five plain signs, posted like crosses in Flanders Field, alerting those of us who have been recklessly impetuous about where we chose to leave our metal steeds when visiting downtown Denman Village, that our amiable and taste-bud tempting little island bakery felt compelled to affirm its right to expect that their mobile customers could comfortably dock their land crafts in front of their place of commerce, sniff the sweet wafting bouquet of fresh bread, pizza and pastries balanced torpidly in the air like invisible honey-smothered butterflies, and stroll a short distance to execute a little economic enhancement.

All very OCP. Still, it's a shame we drove the bakery to it. Promiscuous parking, we now know, can lead to STD's. *(Signs that deter.)* *"They paved paradise and put up a parking lot."* ~ **Joni Mitchell, Big Yellow Taxi.**

The Summation: Once I had decided to write a miniscule gentrification piece on parking lots, it became readily apparent that there are a limited number of useable quotes at my disposal. This may be, in addition to a wide spread belief that parking in general, and parking lots in particular, are an especially uninteresting issue, because they have come to represent, as Joni Mitchell so pungently pointed out, the end of paradise, the end of the road, the end of the frontier. *"They found his ticket book in the trash can on Granville Island. Like he just gave up."* ~ **Character in *"The Delicate Art of Parking,"* a film on, amongst other things, the transformation of the urban parking system.**

Pay parking, should it ever come to Denman, will not garner any respect. And, in any case, the future of pay parking appears to be automation. That'll be the type the *Ferry Corpse* will institute.

I'm not sure I could find the resolve to pay for parking on Denman. There are so many little spots to leave old Nellie in our ersatz commercial core that meters or lots would never appeal to anyone, certainly not to the rough-hewn, back to the land, anarchist parkers *(nosey or not)* who inhabit this semi-tamed land.

Still, the seeds of structured parking have sprouted. The bakery signs…the notice on the Seniors Hall…Islands Trust parking spot requirements…each the insidious beginning of the loss of freedom to park wherever the mood strikes.

Strangers at My Door

"I have always depended on the kindness of strangers." ~ **Blanche Dubois, A Streetcar Named Desire.**

We chatted on a gentle incline one Saturday morning not so long ago, in the heart of the Lindsey-Dickson Wood, on a partially new trail gouged out of a storm-swept hillside leading down to the sweet drinking and swimming water of black-blue Graham Lake. We were a fraction of the volunteer contingent gathering, over what will prove to be an extended period, as we do in communities such as ours, to share communal work, to get whatever jobs need doing, done.

She and I had not met before. A few others were assembled with us on the slope-shifting hillside. Conversation was softly probing, casually candid, not necessarily braided by the hesitation one occasionally resorts to in more public venues. We talked of Island politics, lives and land development, belonging, estrangement, travelling through time, both urban and rural. *"Familiarity breeds contempt-and children."* **Mark Twain, Unpublished Diaries.**

She has been coming to the Island for almost two decades. Her extended family has lived here for at least thirty years. A very long time, I thought. What was oddly transfixing was that she effortlessly described to a stranger her unease, her sense of inaccessibility and that *distance* all the years of visiting the Island had not alleviated, that prickly sensation of forever remaining an alien in one's own land. Her abundance of brief weekends and other vacation visits have not exposed her much to the larger community; she knew of the community but seemed not to have been comfortably drawn close in warm embrace, at least not in the full way one can burrow into the contour of a community by belonging to no other. Though she did not say, she seemed to know that the garb of tourist, of dallier, exerts a caution, throws up a barrier, not necessarily to exclude others, but to rein in garrulous impulses. Sensitive visitors learn how to moderate themselves. *"They'll like you because you're a foreigner. They love foreigners; it's just strangers they hate."* ~ **Jonathan Raban citing a subtle distinction given him on a Mississippi River cruise,** *Old Glory: An American Voyage.*

As we spoke, I thought of my own experience. I first came to Denman Island in 2000. My love and I had searched up and down this chain of solitary links of land for a few years, seeking something, call it a sense of homecoming, an echo of familiar comfort. We could have settled anywhere. Quadra. Lasquiti. Gabriola. As it was, we came here once, toured, returned, explored; a third time, we made an offer on a house. We stayed in three different B&B's, each located in a different part of the Island. We felt accepted, feted in our mercurially acquisitive role, which is somewhat precious to say, I suppose, because we really didn't get to know anyone other than the Real Estate agent and the B&B proprietors until we moved here. We were shoppers, tire kickers, couch hunters. We likely seemed, simultaneously, both hungry and hesitant. For those few we met, we understood that we were simply clients, living, breathing slightly robotic essences of present and potential economic aroma. *"I don't want to play in your yard; I don't like you anymore;"* ~ **Philip Wingate (1894).**

There was a story on the radio recently of growth in a town in the interior. The interviewee lived in a newish, coagulated condo development of some fifty apartments. A huge swath of the owners lived elsewhere. Most of the condos were an investment. Some owners may never have actually seen their purchase. He lamented that it was hard to live in your own home when most of your neighbours were, at best, just passing through. Many of these sorts of holdings are time shares, homes divvied up and owned by a gaggle of strangers, many who intend only to rent the space to another anonymous hodgepodge of short term tenants, a rotating assortment of blissful holidayers who, again, are just passing through.

Is there a lesson here? Some moral paradigm? Likely not. The home as commodity is pretty much a fixture in our society. Still, is it such a leap to suggest healthier communities require their homes to be lived in year round? It becomes embarrassingly awkward, when, for example, places such as Hornby have upwards of sixty percent of its housing owned by off-islanders. Awkward doesn't quite capture it, does it? *"The eyes of strangers are cold like snowdrops."* ~ **Philip Larkin (1922-1986).**

Having been a partial citizen of Denman for seven years now and a full-time resident for the last four, I am beginning to get comfortable with giving 'strangers' the eye, that *'Who the hell are you and how are you going to change my way of life?'* look. I practice in the mirror. First the fake smile, the 'Well, we'll just have to see how you measure up' smirk that belies my panicked fear and concern. Then, the 'Oh, you're an artist *(or writer or whatever trade, profession or esoterically captivating activity I am momentarily enamored of, rely on)* look that makes it all right as long as they enrich me culturally or unplug my creative drain and then move along and leave my life as unruffled as possible. *"I'm so happy to be here. Instead of a hotel full of tourists. Like me."* ~ **Katherine Hepburn's character, Jane Hudson, in the film *'Summertime'*.**

Tourists, those with a healthy measure of day-tripper guilt, must feel that, the sense of walking forever on thin ice. Week-enders as well. Recently a semi-amusing British film star, drolly emphasizing his indolence and need for stimulation, told a talk show host that he needs to take a vacation at least once a week in order to address his spiritual restlessness.

I've never liked being a tourist. Oh, I have certainly enjoyed exotic locations, warm seas and such. But there is something icky and morally unredeemable about being a transient traveler in someone else's sandbox. I sometimes wonder what would happen if we all just stayed put and stopped driving and flying to *Escape Destinations*.

There is a creamy smooth and slick worldly cachet garnered from being a traveler, a person of the world. On the other hand, global warming seems to be nudging us away from the poison of air travel, hastening us, especially those of us with monstrous, puddle-jumper footprints, to give a gander to our own backyard. By that measure, we all should stay put. By another yardstick, these fragile islands might be better preserved if we all just packed up, moved away to the city where our numbers would be quickly absorbed into a density quagmire. *"Never like seein' strangers. Guess it's 'cause no stranger ever good-*

newsed me.” ~ **Walter Brennan's character Groot Nadine as two men on horseback approach from the south in the classic oater, Red River.**

With regard to my 'stranger'ness, likely I'll be dead before I'm fully integrated into this community. Still, I'm of a mind to promote a hale and hearty welcome to one and all who come to our shore. Unlike some, I am not convinced that my way is the best way. Until I gain certainty of my perfection *(again, not likely in this lifetime)* I will treat all people as the good neighbours I expect they are. Until they prove otherwise, of course.

"But Is It …ART?" (Button slogan on the Dental Bus ceiling)

"In art, a dress is never just a dress; nor in life either." ~ Mason Cooley (b. 1927)
U.S. Aphorist.

Of all the undertakings I should gain some facility in, ballroom dancing, languages, mechanics, meditation, weight control, petition selection, tact, art appreciation likely tops the list. I have such a huge deficit in this area that I often have to hold my tongue, with pincer-like care feeling downright unclear as to whether I actually take pleasure in a piece of art. It would be so soothing to say, just once, *'I like what I like'* with conviction!

Alas, bringing myself to a point where I can honestly say 'I like it' about a work of art is far beyond me because, really, once you've said something so definitive, so emphatic, there's always someone in earshot wanting amplification. 'What do you find so appealing in it?' they pummel. 'Huh, what do you REALLY think?' That's where I invariably fall off the rails: the fear of being cornered by a pushy keener.

It wasn't always so. Some years ago, I stumbled across a news item about a meat dress. It was, apparently, a work of art. Housed in Ottawa. 'Where else?' I thought to myself. 'Where else outside of the Senate would an inanimate lump of flesh be held in so high esteem?' But a dress... made of old bossy! I was appalled, having recently begun a dalliance with an unassuming offshoot of vegetarianism.

This dietary conversion, plus my intrinsic art illiteracy, pushed me further into the sinkhole of art barbarism. I wrote a scathing, slyly amusing, little yarn about *the slab of dress* art. I read it to some friends. They said 'you poor

Neanderthal sap. Art is art. Who are you to question the medium?' I said, 'What medium? It's raw meat, for God's sake. It could feed a large family! For a week!!!!' They responded in chorus, tongues tsk tsking, lips clackingly pursed, 'It's food for the soul, you Philistine.'

I withdrew further into my gauche garret. *"Art for art's sake is a philosophy of the well-fed."* ~ **Cao Yu (b.1910) Chinese dramatist.**

As one who can barely draw a straight line, *(even with assistance from a ruler),* I am particularly impressed by the creative process that produces visual art, no matter where I find it. *(Except for meat dresses, I hasten to add. I can't seem to let that go.)* However, before moving to Denman, I went to great lengths to avoid it *(both art and meat clothing),* fearful of having an obviously outlandish opinion surgically extracted from me by some rabidly carnivorous art connoisseur.

Denman, though I suspect it has fewer meat eaters then in times of yore, is, regrettably, rampant with artists and their camp followers. If I was going to live here successfully, I had to take a stab at dealing with my art ignorance.

This is how I came to be an art gallery volunteer. *"Art is dangerous. It is one of the attractions: when it ceases to be dangerous you don't want it."* ~ **Anthony Burgess (1917 - 1993) British Author.**

For the past three years, I have deliberately donated three hours each summer to sit in the art gallery, careful to look knowledgeable, on guard to make sure no one steals or defaces the locally produced artistic expressions. And what a range there is! Some hang. Some stand sentinel on the floor, metal or marble edifices that impress and intimidate, that literally block one's path in the same way clusters of tableau youth occasionally clutter shopping trails in urban malls.

This past year, suffering from debilitating time-management skills, I found myself inadvertently donating a whopping six hours to art exposure. On the first occasion, I was asked if the artist lived on the island. I had failed to attend opening night where artists educate the volunteers and others on their vision. I didn't know the vision. Or the artist. So, I lied. It was a 50/50 gamble that she did live here, even if for the moment. Her watercolours were of Denman. At least I thought they were. They looked pretty shore-like. Soft gentle evocations of sea life. I told myself I liked them. That was as far as it went. After three years, all I had achieved was the ability to mutter to myself my ill-trusted approval.

During my second shift, on behalf of a different artist, I was jittery. Her work exuded menace. It sought to capture the dread, the daring, and the rampage of 2006's formidable winter storms. As an installation, it first needed to be cranked up, set in motion. This required some modest technical manipulation. I failed miserably and had to send out an SOS. The artist, pooch in tow, arrived, handled the electronic buttons I had fumbled, and then departed. I attempted to apologize to her for giving a few patrons the impression that the static rasping out of the small monitor was her attempt to replicate rain on tin roofs. The actual sound effects were of water running over rocks, a much more soothing, if less threatening, aural account than my rash perversion. *"The Art Snob will stand back from a picture at some distance, his head cocked slightly to one side... After a long period of gazing (during which he may occasionally squint his eyes), he will approach to within a few inches of the picture and examine the brushwork; he will then return to his former distant position, give the picture another glance and walk away."* ~ **Russell Lines, *Snobs*, Harper 50.**

I am compelled to snoop on gallery visitors. I inspect their movement, their pensive examination of the work before them, how close they venture to the work in question. They intermittently converse with companions. They whisper. This makes eavesdropping difficult. I resist the urge to suggest that they 'speak-up,' conscious that this might silence them even more. They all look like they 'know' art, with that primal intimacy granted to the chosen few at birth. I am envious. I want to say, 'Share your appreciation with me. Please, I am desperate here. I am adrift.' This would not sound right. I MUST project the impression of total knowledge. I AM an art gallery volunteer. Much is expected of me. *"In other countries, art and literature are left to a lot of shabby bums living in attics and feeding on booze and spaghetti, but in America, the successful writer or artistic painter is indistinguishable from any other decent businessman."* ~ **Sinclair Lewis (1885-1951) U.S. Novelist.**

I would deduce that most of the artists on Denman, though they might prefer to live in attics, by and large, don't. I expect many of them are fond of a swig of wine and some pasta from time to time. The art gallery, though it looks something like a garret, is, in effect, an abandoned handball court. Art SHOULD be hung in a physical place. Imagine how perilous a room it could be if the two uses were combined. The whomping and thudding of a handball denting the space right next to the delicately hung, congenially delicious watercolour or photograph would raise the risk dynamic on gallery hopping a notch or two. Danger would dwell therein: perhaps not in the creation of the art but in its staging, in the war zone of its appreciation. *"The moment you think you understand a great work of art, it's dead for you."* ~ **Robert Wilson (b. 1941) U.S. Theater director.**

Another summer of art custodianship has since ended. I suspect that I am, unlike the other volunteers, not much more than a security guard. I am here to keep the artist's work safe. This is my mission. Though I have attempted, when asked, to offer 'opinions', to step outside my comfort zone, this is not a legitimate direction for me to go. I simply do not understand the purpose of art. And even if I do, I am uneasy about the depth of my opinion. Silence is a more fitting route. And perhaps less awkward for one and all.

Hit In the Eye With a Sharp Poker Hand

"There are two great pleasures in gambling; that of winning and that of losing."
~ **French proverb.**

My parents liked to gamble. With machines, primarily. Machines...and keno-like tickets. A compelling black and white photo of my parents hangs just before the door to my wine cellar. In it, they are glowingly smiling with their trusted companion, a Vegas (or Reno, perhaps) slot machine. I sometimes think of that slot (any slot) as the brother I never had. Such was the intensity of my parent's addiction.

My mother was a saver. Gambling, for her, was grounded in her impoverished childhood. It meant, if anything, that she could dabble with 'acceptable risk'. My father had a slightly different perspective. His uncle lost a ranch in a poker game back in the early part of the last century. His family credo became 'never play cards for money'. My pop was a stickler on this subject.

Of late, being a child (and an unfortunate adult) completely obsessed by the TUBE, I have been taken by TV poker games and free internet gambling. I appear to have jumped in to my weakened genetic pool. Not too long ago, I briefly joined a poker collective. *"Someone once asked me why women don't gamble as much as men do, and I gave the common-sensical reply that we don't have as much money. That was a true but incomplete answer. In fact, women's total instinct for gambling is satisfied by marriage."* ~ **Gloria Steinem, 'Night Thoughts of a Media Watcher', Ms. Magazine November 1981.**

These small social slip-ups happen so matter-of-factly. A guest in my house one night idly mentions his recent predilection for cards. The game happens weekly. He is a social fellow, much more rounded than I. I prefer solitary entertainments. I do recognize, however, that it would be healthier if I stepped outside that inhibiting cloak once in a while. At the same time, my parent's preoccupation with gambling flashes before my memory's eyes. I hesitate.

They stayed at home to raise my sister and me. Once we were out the door, *(which was not a smooth transition as my sister, unlike yours truly who bailed early and often, maintained a long umbilical affinity for the perks of home life,)* they became social gadflies. They played bingo six or seven nights a week for years. They went to Reno ten times a year. They had the good graces not to invite me. They had done their job with me. And they continued to save me from myself by not inflicting the beauty and the horror of gaudy gambling spots on me. My sister went on occasion but I deferred and only once entered the valley of lost souls, Las Vegas.

Groot:	*"Now wait a minute, Quo. You really ain't gonna take a man's only set a teeth, are ya?"*
Quo:	*"Uh huh."*
Groot:	*"Yeah, but I gotta use 'em for eatin.'*
Quo:	*"Come grub you get 'em."*
Groot:	*"What ya' gonna do with 'em?"*
Quo:	*"My name now Two-Jaw Quo."*

Groot Nadine (portrayed by Walter Brennan and Quo, (portrayed by Chief Yowlatchie) in the oater Red River after Groot loses his teeth to Quo in a poker game (1948).

Some years ago, my partner and I drove to New Mexico to visit family. This journey coincided with one of my parent's interminable attempts to gamble away my inheritance. They invited us to drop in to Vegas on our drive back. We came in by the backdoor, through arid desert and boiling heat. We passed over the giant Hoover Dam, an incongruous edifice needed to power the massive waste of electricity that fuels the gambling Mecca. We hooked up with my small-town parents in their true element, the gaudy, slightly excessive, three star Four Queens Hotel. People were making small wagers even as they stood in line to register. Every place we went, to eat, to be entertained, to walk, the opportunity to wage money thrust its provocative loins in our face. I retreated to my bed. The next day, I could not get out of town fast enough. *"The action is everything, more consuming than sex, more immediate than politics, more important always than the acquisition of money, which is never, for the gambler, the true point of the exercise."* ~ **Joan Didion, U.S. Essayist.**

For reasons not solely pertaining to the lure of gambling, I have retreated from my short-lived enthusiasm for poker. There are some personal pleasures that I am compelled to engage in over and over. Poker, gambling, socializing with others for the primary purpose of lightening their pockets is not for me.

And neither, really, was it my parents' style. Admittedly, they were drawn to the inspirational lights of Vegas, that asylum of besotted gaming incomprehensibility. But I think, even more than the gambling, they yearned for, found joy in, the journey there and back. They would pack food and drink and little inflatable pillows for their aging tushes, board the bus at a Vancouver Hotel, and journey south. Often, my sister and I, and our respective families, would have dinner with my parents just before their departure. My father would buy, big time spender that he occasionally was. Aside from Christmas, this was often our primary family activity, my father buoyant with the anticipation of bus travel, and I suppose seeing his kids, and my mother, adoring every moment, the routine of their lives. The pleasure was in the repetition of gestures guaranteed to offer consistent payback. They made that bus journey south dozens of times. We met for dinner almost as frequently. These were precious and passing moments as the years had their way with my small family. *"Playing poker in their Quonset hut on Tinian, killing the last hours of the preatomic age."* ~**Peter Goldman: Commenting on US bomber crew scheduled to carry the first atomic bomb, 'Newsweek 29 Jul 85'.**

As resistant as I am to being drawn into the genteel pastime of a friendly game of cards, I am occasionally up for it. Partly, I am trying to avoid becoming my father. In his last years, he refused to play cards in the care home in which he was compelled to live. His decade's old vow never to play cards for money kept him away from penny-ante socializing in the games room. He eschewed in-house bingo because it seemed to him to be an act of betrayal to my mother, finding no delight in any of the activities they had shared together. He also drew the line at shooting pool with me. For him the journey was coming to an end. He was just waiting it out, undeterred by any transitory distractions. He had but one more departure of note and, with a little luck, though we didn't bet on it, one final arrival.

Missing Manners - That's Ma'am, as in Ham

"He is the very pineapple of politeness!" ~ **Richard Sheridan (1751-1816) dramatist.**

It is fortuitous that, upon planning to move to Denman Island, I temporarily forgot that a similarly sized population passed away in fanatical harmony in Jonestown a few decades earlier. Otherwise, I might have shied away from planting myself here in this smallish community. But there was no need to worry. Pigs will fly, or at least take an Alaskan cruise, before this issue-ridden, conflict-driven community will ever coalesce sufficiently to swill the communal venom of compulsive agony.

Still, even with the lurking threat of demise by conformity, I am tempted to gingerly raise the subject of how we treat each other, both in person and in print, on this island. Being so new to these sparkling shores, it may be presumptuous for me to call our behavioral customs into question. Alas, I am foolishly brash and sufficiently unsettled by the snappish regimen of name-calling, verbal defecation and metaphorical malapropism that someone has to spew and, if not I, then who? No doubt a thus far closeted Ann Landers clone will tell me, either in a mass e-mailing, a Grapevine insert or a corporally punitive, lecturing letter to the Flagstone editor. Be advised that I fully accept whatever comeuppance comes my way. *"Nobody thanks a witty man for politeness when he accommodates himself to a society in which it is not polite to display wit."* ~ **Nietzsche (1844-1900) Philosopher and Scholar.**

I am aware that my sardonic gibes and occasionally obscure humour, which some call wit and others call witless, has often befuddled or inflamed some on this moated Isle. In that sense, I am not innocent of sharpness, of pointed barb.

71

I do like to think that I am sufficiently obtuse that the sting of my whittling wit is lessened some. I have always preferred to meander around the grassy knoll of controversy rather than shoot to the heart of the matter. *"The Japanese have perfected good manners and made them indistinguishable from rudeness."* ~ **Paul Theroux (b. 1941) Travel Writer.**

How we deal with disagreement and conflict demonstrates what sort of community we have. For example, the recent Local Trust decision engendered a conventional reaction. This reaction, which mostly took the form of a petition, itself fashioned a swarm of severe censure. Much sniping occurred via e-mail and the more archetypal leaflet insert. Leaflets seem to me to be such a constricted means of communication. While some can be constructed in pleasant and thoughtful language, the very limitations of language can invariably win out. Points are often made more harshly than necessary: the intent is not only to chastise but to conscript.

Letters and inserts have attempted to admonish, to embarrass, to lecture and deride, to, in effect, direct people to the correct position. It would seem that some in our midst know what that correct position is. This is of immeasurable help. Often those of us on the erroneous side of an issue are blindly entrenched: We are thought to welcome the charitable bid to repent, to undo, to return to the correct fold *(or staple or mutilate.)* *"We have had to agree on a certain set of rules, called etiquette and politeness, to make this frequent meeting tolerable and that we need not come to open war. We meet at the post-office, and at the sociable, and about the fireside every night; we live thick and are in each other's way, and stumble over one another, and I think that we lose some respect for one another. Certainly less frequency would suffice for all important and hearty communications.* ~ **Henry David Thoreau (1817-1862 Author and Naturalist.**

Language can be used as a weapon by professional pamphleteers and the like to coerce others to accept a different position, or to reinforce positions held. As a satirist, I recognize the lethal, or injurious, bite of language. Language bears some metaphorical similarity to the fists of a pugilist. I am not nor have I ever been a boxer *(except for one misguided Saturday afternoon in my mid-teens when I dropped into the Nanaimo Boxing Club which was, in those long ago days located in the basement of some forgotten Nanaimo pub, but that is another story.)* I much prefer the role of jester. Rarely am I tempted to counter-punch another to change their mind on a particular subject. The individual has the inalienable right, to my way of thinking, to believe whatever they wish. I think it more civilized to 'agree to disagree.' Not as humourous, but more civil. *"I have always been of the mind that in a democracy manners are the only effective weapons against the bowie-knife."* ~ **James Russell Lowell (1819-1891) Poet.**

As a newcomer, and someone who has, over a lifetime, willingly signed countless petitions, I have never seen such energy devoted to encouraging thoughtful people to withdraw from a position. I hesitate to say that it smacks of bullying but am hard pressed to coin another term. Having made this rather provocative assessment, I am at a loss as to the correct forum within which to explore my conclusion. By nature not being an inserter, and requiring more than the one-way communication leaflets and letters engender, I have chosen my usual route; *'the column'*. I am grateful to have this means: one available to anyone I suppose who would choose to access it.

The point of this essay is really nothing more than to express sadness at the recent torrent of rhetoric *(most of it was hammering rather than discourse)*. I am bewildered that such a small community cannot find other means to politely and respectfully engage in dialogue. The cacophony of badgering that has reared up and torn at the weathered social fabric of this island is a bitter and intolerant dissonance, and certainly not debate in the least. We would do well to dispatch it. *"My generation of radicals and breakers-down never found anything to take the place of the old virtues of work and courage and the old graces of courtesy and politeness."* ~ **F. Scott Fitzgerald (1896-1940) Author in a letter to his daughter in 1938.**

Many of us come from the vocational battlefields of universities, business and labour. Others have fought *(and still do fight)* in the armies of protest and resistance. Bloodletting is an integral by-product of that zeal. The struggles are always intense, the passions unrelenting.

If you listen to old-timers rhapsodically reminisce about early days on Denman, days not unlike the present, days ever dogged by the machinery of change, the conflict and spite we now experience is not that much different. The lick may vary; the undercurrent may have flown more true once. But the spine of the matter is as bent out of shape as ever.

73

As ingrained as it may have been, still is by most accounts, warrior ardor does not belong in a small village. The very fact that we are a relatively contained community should allow us, bearing in mind Thoreau's counsel, sufficient opportunity to discuss one on one or in assembly any difference of opinion.

Of course, divisiveness has its advantages. How better to resist change than to huddle in our separate caves, stepping out from time to time to shew away intruders and throw the odd bit of prickly bric-a-brac at them as they scurry into the woods.

Homeward Bind

"Home is a notion that only nations of the homeless fully appreciate and only the uprooted comprehend." ~ **Wallace Stegner.**

Over half a decade ago, in the waning months of 2007, I helped organize two 'speak-outs' on housing. Against a backdrop of possible, but highly unlikely, munificence being squeezed out of the Denman Island OCP *(Official Community Plan)* via a review, Erin O'Brien-Hornsey and I, at the time, the only two Denman members of ISLA, a fledgling Land Trust *(now exclusively dedicated to Hornby's affordable housing struggle)*, agreed to host two get-togethers to make an effort to get at the hush-hush world of affordable housing on Denman — *I say hush-hush because it sounds warm and cuddly, even though I mean clandestine.*

Anecdotal evidence suggested that there were, and no doubt still are, an indeterminate number of people on Denman who live in some form of prohibited or non-approved housing. This is not much different from most anywhere else in the world. Housing is a commodity, a product. Most people need it. Some people play fast and loose with it. Buyers and sellers! Owners and renters! The way of the world! *"It is a curious emotion, this certain homesickness I have in mind. With Americans, it is a national trait, as native to us as the rollercoaster or the jukebox. It is no simple longing for the home town or country of our birth...as often as not, we are homesick most for the places we have never known."* ~ **Carson McCullers (1917–1967), U.S. author. "Look Homeward, Americans," Vogue (New York, Dec. 1, 1940).**

My parents owned a hardscrabble motel for some of my impressionable years. We catered to, for the most part, transient and semi-permanent tenants, people who might stay for a day, a week or, perhaps, a couple of months at most. I do not have fond memories of being the one providing shelter for people. There was something uncomfortable about it, about having people pay for parcels of space that you owned. Some of the patrons of the U-Rest Auto Court took off in the middle of the night. Sometimes they left their possessions, as if to say, "Will that cover what we owe?"

I would paw through these abandoned items, boxes of books, odds and ends, their private stuff. I came to believe that people should hang on to their gear, that I had no business rummaging through the bits and pieces of their lives they had left behind. By the same token, I wondered how people could just up and leave the things you expect them to value. Eventually, I learned that sometimes people have few choices, few, and sometimes none. *"There are things you just can't do in life. You can't beat the phone company, you can't make a waiter see you until he's ready to see you, and you can't go home again."* ~ **Bill Bryson (b. 1951), U.S. author, and journalist. The Lost Continent: Travels in Small Town America, chapter 2 (1989).**

When I choose to, which is rarely, I can drive by all the houses I lived in growing up. There aren't that many. At this precise moment in time, all three *(including the iconic but worn down U Rest)* still stand, three, I should note, *if* you don't count my parent's small fish boat that doubled as my crib and their means of staying economically afloat for the first year of my life.

Across the street from my parent's last house, and by that I mean the home that they last lived in together, the home my mother left when she entered the hospital where she died, the home we extracted my father from in order to move him into a cheery institution *(one of two he had the questionable fortune to occupy before he went to another hospital to die,)* there used to stand four houses of some significant ancestry. They were not heritage homes, the name generally bestowed on venerable and ancient buildings. They were, however, more than just creaky old relics. They were built at the turn of the last century as homes for colliers and their large families. When I knew these houses, walked by them, delivered newspapers to their doors, for I can't recall ever being invited inside, I had little interest in antiquity, in the history of houses and homes. *"I grew up in this town, my poetry was born between the hill and the river, it took its voice from the rain, and like the timber, it steeped itself in the forests.* " ~ **Pablo Neruda, on viewing his childhood home of Temuco, Argentina, as he fled a new political regime in Chile, *Wall Street Journal* 14 Nov 85.**

I recently drove on that street where my parents last lived. It was as it always was, a short street cramped between the railway tracks and a scar of a major artery that, then, as now, slashes through much of Nanaimo in many spots, especially just north of the sixty-year-old George S. Pearson Bridge, which crosses the Millstream River. The quartet of old houses, which once looked across at my parent's home, was gone. In their stead, a bare patch of jumbled earth waited. Nearby, a new Ramada Inn, another in a long list of low rent motels that have been blighting, or enhancing, if you will, the neighborhood of my long ago since the 1960's, had been erected. *"Compromise makes a good umbrella but a poor roof."* ~ **James Russell Lowell (1819–1891), U.S. poet, editor. From a speech, Oct. 6, 1884, Birmingham, England, "On Democracy."**

Much time has passed since our two speak-outs. Affordable Housing has tiptoed into the lexicon of popular culture in a way one might easily have expected. On Denman, there has been some modest to-do, but not much else, about the need. DCLTA, a hard-working group to be sure, has been created. There has been discussion, political positioning, a survey, an extended zoning adjustment, and much practiced caution. Significant time has been spent, or withered, crafting the ubiquitous Housing Agreement. Lawyers have been at work, thank the Lord.

We are, in August of 2013, on the threshold of more to-do. A second Housing Group has been unveiled, The Denman Housing Association. A survey of need is afoot. Additionally, The LTC is holding a Cooking Up Housing Policy hot-dog eating contest later on in August, which sounds vaguely nutritious until you remember that this is not a fast-food Island and that the colloquial meaning of to 'cook up' something is to fabricate and concoct. There are people of good will here. We have an out-of-whack population curve. Everyone thinks they know the answer. Hopefully, we'll get beyond talking it to death

Arrivals and Departures (Comings and Goings): *A Manifesto of Sorts.*

"A farmer, a hunter, a soldier, a reporter, even a philosopher, may be daunted; but nothing can deter a poet, for he is actuated by pure love. Who can predict his comings and goings? His business calls him out at all hours, even when doctors sleep. ~ **Henry David Thoreau, (1817-1862), Walden (1954)**

Since disembarking on these sporadically cantankerous shores, I have gazed, naively perhaps, navelly possibly, nonsensically to be sure, at my new Island home with the eyes of a new, if somewhat aging, lover. How else should one approach one's new territory, one's home, perhaps, for the balance of life? My world view has suffered radical realignment since departing the profoundly overpopulated Lower Mainland. There, I was an inconspicuous creature. I shuffled along in the shadows, a foot-dragging city slouch who came and went wherever I thought I ought to with no one particularly aware of me, no one the wiser about my movements. Occasionally, in some small circle of endeavor, I stepped into a faint floodlight. However, the millions of folks who might see me on any given day had no true inkling of me.

Here, in the so-called solitude of Ruraltania, it is as plain as the toes on my tootsies that it was the city that protected me, that offered a thousand cloaks of anonymity. Here, I am one of a few. Exercising my primal urge to write nonsense, I have been resurrected with a faintly flickering glow. I have tramped into a frightful firmament, every foolish footfall a potentially irreversible leg hold trap of tiny town terror. *"Looking back is a bad habit"* ~ **Rooster Cogburn (John Wayne) in *True Grit.***

One winter day, a day apparently reserved for the exploits of the semi-mythical groundhog, I did a visioning committee stint at the recycling depot.

This place is surely a repository of fleeting arrivals and departures. My task was to inveigle islanders to jot down their dreams for the future of this island on a sticky note. Alas, the poster came without the sticky notes and none could be had.

I became a barker but had little inclination for the work. It was a chilly morning and the streams of recyclers were possessed by speed and urgency. They were people on a mission, a trudging swirl of dutiful drudgery, and seemed to have little truck for futuristic claptrap.

As my neighbours lugged their baskets of recyclables to the various stations, a twinkle-eyed, island elder was carted off to an adjacent field by his preciously precocious pooch. The slavish elder winged a ball from a plastic launcher. It soared through the air to a landing. The vibrating dog retrieved the ball and fetched it back to its master. He winged it again, coming and going, over and over. This ball ballet is, he says, a daily ritual. Within the chosen space, anywhere they want really, they, man and mutt, regurgitate in play, a play that will repeat itself as long as their respective stamina's allow. *"If we are arriving and departing, it is also true that we are eternally anchored. One's destination is never a place but rather a new way of looking at things."* ~ **Henry Miller (1891-1980) Author, "The Oranges of the Millennium".**

The urban rush, the glass concrete and steel metropolicity, the brace of mammoth bridges connecting disparate communities, all of it can give one the false notion of total liberty. Hanging over the heads of Lower Mainlanders, like some fearsome bureaucratic guillotine, is the terrible promise of toll booths the government intends to wreak on them. Freedom's movement will be shackled by a travel tax travesty. Some will pay, some will not.

Island living, with its ferry toll, is not so different. I have sequestered myself away from much of the hustle and bustle *(though I still have an eye for a well-turned bustle),* a calculated choice to extricate myself from unnecessary travel, to escape urban fluster. I know from observing myself that I like the stillness of my own thoughts, the peace of immobility. I admit to also enjoying the static pleasures of electronically transmitted signals, of exploring the almost imaginary gypsy world of television and the web in a cosset of seclusion. But I have limits, and the draw of human interaction hauls me out from time to time, out from my lair, into the company of folks.

These comings and goings require doggedness. As inverted as islanders appear to be, there are, to my reckoning, limitless opportunities to socialize. Cultural events overflow. Artists and musicians abound. In the public arena, they flourish. In private, I imagine they blossom. *"Conventional people are roused to fury by departures from convention, largely because they regard such departures as a criticism of themselves."* ~ **Bertrand Russell (1872–1970), British philosopher, mathematician. The Conquest of Happiness, chapter 9 (1930).**

Though I am hardly a self-sufficient person, *(my survival skills are admittedly inner-city in scope and even then, they were barely adequate),* I convince myself from day to day that I can manage this rustic enclave. Challenges abound, nevertheless. There are prescribed ways of being, of doing: country etiquette that subsists in the memory of all who were here before and those more recent arrivals who seem like they were always here. These human expectations need to be prodded out, like the shiny nuggets they are.

On these shores, one also needs to discover how to be mindful of the seasons, of their arrivals and departures. They reach into your soul with an intensity not learned in the city. Slowly, awkwardly, I begin to observe the subtle shift of wind and weather: flock after flock of birds winging north in V waves, skimming in dazzling formation mere inches above the ocean.

Even though an awful urban anxiety still flows in my veins, a fluttering perseverance not unlike that of the elders vibrating mutt, I continue to try to wind down, to be at peace in this pleasant rural courtyard I have travelled to.

Libraries, Health Care and the Beaver

"A man's library is a sort of harem." ~ **Ralph Waldo Emerson (1803–1882), poet, philosopher.**

As I recuperated from knee surgery not so long ago, I spent a wobble of time considering my health. One morning, near the end of my modest recuperation, I watched, as was my seductive inclination then, an episode of LITB *(Leave it to Beaver)*. As a keen, albeit amateur library volunteer, I was especially ensnared by this particular chapter of the Beav's wondrous life story. It dawns with Beaver Cleaver browsing through his father's home library, a comfortable middle-class parlour circa 1960. In my home, growing up, we had no library nor, for that matter, bookshelves. Instead, my parents usually had a book or magazine circulating on their respective night tables often as not next to the containers where their false teeth soaked overnight. My folks also kept the odd picture book on the coffee table. As I grew to adolescence, they acquired additional picture books, a 1912 encyclopedia set *(it came with a house we bought,)* and intermittent second-hand National Geographic's *(and, of course, innumerable copies of Readers Digest);* no doubt all were meant to broaden the skimpy horizon afforded me and my sister in the borstal-like confines of Nanaimo. In later times, these gems of mass-produced bookbinding were enhanced by my carefully considered, obligatory Christmas offerings, coffee-table epics to be stacked and occasionally thumbed through down the coming years. On reflection, my mom and dad were probably less than habitual readers. Mom collected newspaper recipes. In later years, my dad drifted down the dark streets of crime fiction, courtesy of my sister's reading habits. I have no actual memory of either of my parental units sitting down with a 'good book,' plunging into some imagined world. It may have happened

81

but their real world wouldn't have afforded them much time for such luxuries. Their experience would have shushed the inclination. *"Every library should try to be complete on something, if it were only the history of pinheads."* ~ **Oliver Wendell Holmes, Sr. (1809–1894), U.S. writer, physician.**

In the episode I viewed, Beaver has a grade four book report due. Ward loans him his library card. Improbably, it is plastic and resembles a credit card. As this show was set at the tail end of the 1950's, a time barely preceding credit cards, this early use of plastic somewhat confounded me.

Anyway, The Library in Mayfield, their fictional town, is named after a deceased VIP whose name I didn't catch. In stone etching, above the entrance way, the sign also says FREE PUBLIC LIBRARY. Not just a public library but a *'FREE'* Public Library.

Now we know that Libraries are not truly 'free.' Taxes pay for them. Our taxes! There is, I believe, consensus that reading should be promoted, that people should not be constrained in accessing books. Americans in the fifties, not to say now, would likely bridle at the notion that free access to books is a tad socialistic. So, we don't point it out unless we really want to irritate them. Yet when health care is mentioned…there…by Republicans usually…but also by complicit Democrats…free access to health care, a grand gesture we still have here in Canada *(though some think it on shaky ground,)* is smacked with the soubriquet of socialism.

In Beaver's world, there is health care for his family. Doctors make home visits. The world is well-ordered. The Library sings out loudly that it is FREE! FREE!! Good God Almighty, FREE!!! *"Time rushes toward us with its hospital tray of infinitely varied narcotics, even while it is preparing us for its inevitably fatal operation."* ~ **Tennessee Williams (1914–1983).**

As I enter my final couple of decades *(and here I may be displaying way too much confidence)* I live on an Island *(entirely of my own doing, I'm not blaming anyone)* which has no Public Library *(yet)* and, whilst it has an admirable little nomadic clinic, a community project painfully close to having a permanent home, no Hospital. I've already chalked up two annoying surgeries of no major upshot and one with quite a bit more intrusion into my unadventurous life. I can sense the hovering imminence of unremitting medical intervention.

Recently, I attended the thirtieth anniversary AGM of the Hornby & Denman Community Health Care Society. As I listened to the march of reports, the tassels of common history shared, I began to appreciate, in a way I hadn't before, that these two Islands have a depth of organizational acumen, born out of necessity, which one simply doesn't encounter in the city. The city has infrastructure galore. Piddly islands craft what they need over a lengthy period of time.

My point, as elusive to me as it likely is to you, dear reader, is that I am now paying much closer attention to the world around me, especially as it worms its way into my remaining years. *"One has but to observe a community of beavers at work in a stream to understand the loss in his sagacity, balance, co-operation, competence, and purpose which Man has suffered since he rose up on his hind legs.... He began to chatter and he developed Reason, Thought, and Imagination, qualities which would get the smartest group of rabbits or orioles in the world into inextricable trouble overnight."* ~ **James Thurber (1894–1961), U.S. humorist, illustrator. "Thinking Ourselves Into Trouble."**

But back to Clinics, Libraries, Beavers and such, really, all of the bric-a-brac of infrastructure which Denman Island displays, has evolved from its own bucket list of systems over the years. There are environmental groups, large, small, influential, home-spun; there is a health system, with two organizations devoted to a range of health services and a community-minded bevy of medical practitioners. This does not include the entrepreneurial specialists who provide a selection of other health services.

The fire department is an esteemed and capable constituent. We have an underfunded wealth of communal gathering spots, the Hall, the Other Hall, the Old School, sort of a partitioned Hall, the elementary school, which has meeting chambers and an actual hall-way. The Arts flourish both in structured and scrambled fashion. Some congregate in the Arts Centre which is no slouch itself as a cute little refurbished Hall.

As marvelous as it all is, there is, some would argue, *(and don't some of us like to quibble),* room for improvement. Others might contend that I should have moved to some real-life facsimile of Beaver's back lot home, my own mythic Mayfield. I posit that I, a minor, light-weight prognosticator, have already done so. To my way of thinking, Denman is *(or at least was)* Mayfield...not so long ago. I'll go to my soggy green grave thinking that.

83

A 'How-I-Learned-To-Work-Then-Leave-It-All-Behind' Reminiscence

"I had to quit my taxi cab driving job because I had no way to get to work. The problem was I kept calling myself to come pick me up." ~ **Jarod Kintz.**

An early episode of *Leave it to Beaver* has the Beaver, age ten, and Wally, age twelve, sharing a newspaper route with fifty-eight customers. They get the job in order to earn money to buy bikes. Their job is not arduous! I should know. I traipsed lightly as a paper boy for four years, from age eleven to fifteen with, on average, sixty plus customers. I did my route *(I was Route 66, incidentally, so I was thrilled to see the TV show come to the airwaves half-way through my paperboy exploits)* on my lonesome. I didn't have a younger brother tagging along. I did have a kid sister, but she wasn't all that collaborative.

Like the Beav and Wally, I had drive. Of course, I *did* subcontract out Mondays for most of those four years. Mondays, I bowled! Five pin! I embraced, at a young age, a healthy work-play balance. In the fifties, there was great promise of much leisure time. I wanted to be ready. Alas, the Beaver and Wally survive a little over a week in the news delivery game: actually, twenty-six minutes of real time. They lose their position because Ward, their papa, doesn't trust them. He and mama June step in pre-emptively, without consulting the young entrepreneurs, and deliver the wrong Saturday papers, expired leftovers from the previous week! The lads are discharged because of interfering parental units! Ward makes amends in the end, gets them their job back by explaining what a meddling doofus he is, but, by then, his sons have

84

moved on. They are off to see about getting a job at a supermarket. Packing boxes! An indoor job! *"I believe that if a man does a job as well as a woman, he should be paid as much."* ~ **Celeste Holm.**

The synchronicity for me is stupefying. I am relating like crazy. A few months after my paperboy days, I scored a job stocking shelves at a supermarket. Butterfingers that I was, I dropped copious glass jars of ketchup in those long-ago, mostly pre-plastic days. The linoleum was regularly splattered with shards of glass and oozing buckets of blood-red condiment. During my apprenticeship, I had deftly manhandled all sorts of glass food products with a juggler's dexterity. Unfortunately, that knack didn't translate under fire. Like some gory theatre of war, the floors of the Nanaimo Safeway on Townsite Road ran crimson pretty much on my every shift. I was doomed.

Subsequently, a red-brick, corner grocery store down the street from my house took a chance on my measly stocking skills. There was less of a factory feel to this job. I hung on to it for most of that year. The pace was manageable, damage was modest. *"Working cuts down on both folly and wisdom."* ~ **Mason Cooley (b. 1927) U.S. aphorist.**

As I watched the LITB episode that one winter's day, I began to wonder if anything I had ever done was truly original. Did my life somehow navigate in the same watery script-canal written for the Beav and his artificial family tree?

After my four-year stint delivering the Nanaimo Daily Free Press, and before my two sojourns in the food retail racket, I worked briefly for a chiropractor. He had a business empire that included a soda fountain and a toy store along with his practice. I was fifteen and naively convinced myself that I had found my life's target. With my considerable business flair, honed from four solid years of stick handling fiddly route collection payment requirements, not to mention the generous tips I was sometimes given, clearly because I was a crackerjack, freckle-faced capitalist and budding sycophantic salesman, I was poised to take up my true calling in the kick-ass world of commerce. *"If my films make one more person miserable, I'll feel I have done my job."* ~ **Woody Allen.**

The job with Dr. Bone-Cruncher lasted a summer. I was sacked for playing with the toys. Which toys I can't remember. Likely, they were not age appropriate. But it wasn't the toys and their allure that did me in and ruined my career trajectory. Nah! It was the windows. The pre-Bill Gates kind. I could not avoid leaving streaks on the windows I was assigned to clean, the ones that faced the street and showed people what great coffee and milkshakes we made. The ones that also displayed and tempted one and all to buy our toys and other confections. To this day, I still don't do windows well. It's a habit I can't break.

"When I quit working, I lost all sense of identity in about fifteen minutes."
~ **Paige Rense (b. 1929), U.S. author and editor, recalling her brief period of being a housewife.**

What I really started to write about in this column *(and obviously got side-tracked from early on)* was that sense of bereavement that accompanies the end of a career. It is akin to giving up smoking. Even though I haven't smoked the noxious weed in over a quarter of a century, I still crave the grungy taste and smoky-fire flavour of cigarettes.

Every once in a while, I want to go back to work. I was a social worker. As stupidly mindless as the bureaucracy was that I found myself in, good and meaningful labour was possible. I have written a novel about it which will be released shortly. Initially I wrote *'Like a Child to Home'*, I believed, to purge my lingering work demons. I now think it was to resurrect them, to savour them once again. For me, work was always about the people who shared my journey. That is what I miss most. These days, I sometimes watch TV in order to catch a glimpse of how people doing work are portrayed. I feast on gorgeous worksite interplay. Cop shows that illustrate the nitty-gritty of work demands and relationships most closely match my idealized memory of my abandoned work world.

Lost in this voyeuristic mix of simulated work situations and memories of early entrepreneurial yearnings are my derailed tycoon impulses. A chance friendship with a lovely family of leafleting communists and the sizzling political furnace that was SFU circa 1965 ruined me for corporate ascendancy. I could no more hang on to those business dreams than I could grip those elusive bottles of sugary Heinz relief.

But I still think about work, about my lifelong orientation to it, my continued bemusement by it, my forever exile from it.

My Musical Career

"Dylan used to sound like a lung cancer victim singing Woody Guthrie. Now he sounds like a Rolling Stone singing Immanuel Kant." ~ **Quoted in Robert Shelton, No Direction Home, ch. 2, "Prophet Without Honor" (1986). Twin City a Go-Go (Minneapolis, 1965)**

I don't often dwell on my musical career. Primarily because I didn't have one. This is not to say that I haven't sung my heart out from time to time in a few hot spots. Aside from warbling to the sound of old 78's twirling on the combination record player radio consul my parents bought at the local Eaton's store in Nanaimo, especially pseudo-yodeling along with Wilf Carter *(aka Montana Slim)* and his inimitable, tragic classic, *'One Golden Curl'*, my first public singing experience, was at the local Mormon Church. My mother came from Anglican stock: my father had Latter-Day Saint's roots. Their religious trappings were thinly threaded. In time, mom and dad, as a character-building initiative, parceled me and my sister out to the LDS Sunday School up the street. Though there was a pot of pious pablum, there was also singing. Belting out hymns was good fun. I jumped in with both lungs. Mormonism, like many full-of-beans religions, likes to lace the air with historic, histrionic hymns. I rallied round many a rousing religious refrain. I wasn't an especially celestial crooner but the congregated voices of the small parish were stirring.

In my tweens, to give life more balance, I fleetingly ventured across town to the Victoria Road Gospel Hall. Unlike the moderately animated Mormons, the Gospelites were jumping-out-of-their-seats singing fanatics. The joint hopped, though the sacred messages sometimes weighed the proceedings down. *"Looking foolish does the spirit good. The need not to look foolish is one of youth's many burdens; as we get older we are exempted from them more and more, and float upward in our heedlessness, singing Gratia Dei sum quod sum."* ~ **John Updike (b. 1932), U.S. author, critic. Self-Consciousness: Memoirs, ch. 6 (1989).**

In Junior High, I signed up for the school choir. An easy music class credit you'd think. Up to then, the sum total of my formal musical training consisted of a brief bellow of flutophone training in Grade five. Being a goof-off at an early age, I was summarily dismissed from that class *(taught by a local music store clerk who either didn't know how to teach or unreasonably expected compliant and breathless Wunderkinds)* for incessant chatter. Negotiations to reinstate me ensued but nothing came of it.

This penchant for disrupting the proceedings followed me into the school choir. Even the pleasing grandeur of my tremendous adolescent-soprano-verging-on-tenor voice could not redeem me in the eyes of the choirmaster *(who, in any case, I suspected was a kissing cousin of my flutophone grand inquisitor.)* I continued my clowning around ad nauseam and was finally given a righteous if overly repressive boot. *"Love, I find, is like singing. Everybody can do enough to satisfy themselves, though it may not impress the neighbours as being very much."* ~ **Zora Neale Hurston (1891–1960), African-American novelist, short story writer, folklorist, playwright and anthropologist. 'Dust Tracks on a Road', ch. 14, J.P. Lippincott (1942).**

In my sixteenth year, I began to have grave doubts about the validity of a key Mormon tenet which held that, eons earlier, a submarine had crossed the sea from Asia to populate the virgin shores of North America with a people who would transform into the First Nations folk to whom we now owe significant reparations. Curbing my rush of religious probing was the appearance of a new member of the flock. I was taken with this comely lass even though she was a few years older than me. Daughter of the new High School Music teacher, she brought an urbane mystery to our little congregation. In the church at the same time, there were two young family men who played guitar and dreamt of putting together a small Christian folk group. My soon-to-be notorious inamorata, economically caged at home to redraft an earlier, failed foray into the cruel world, the two howling, domestically entrenched hootenanians, and me, barely able to carry a tune but oh so enamoured of my older woman, formed a small quartet the name of which I have chosen to forget. It may have been the Foreplays but who can remember.

In any event, we practiced for a number of months. Our betwixted foursome, marinated in undeclared pressures, strained with religious unease, connubial demands and sexual tension. Predictably, we disbanded, un-unveiled, underwhelming, unconsummated. My dalliance with my older woman ended in cowardly fashion. I caved in to the natter of peers who scoffed at the experience I was undergoing. *"In a house where there are small children the bathroom soon takes on the appearance of the Old Curiosity Shop."* ~ **Robert Benchley (1889–1945), U.S. writer, humorist. The Treasurer's Report and Other Aspects of Community Singing, "The Bathroom Revolution," Grosset & Dunlap (1930).**

I left my small town. The years went by. I joined that cheerless convention of vague and aging vocalists who drone to the radio *(or more current musical/automobile technologies)* or who are left no option but to belt out the same jingle over and over again in the shower. Not blessed with the most efficient memory, my shower song of choice and necessity has usually been "Shenandoah." A lament for a lost love, it has been my constant companion as I search for the ideal scrubbing. *"The first time I sang in the Church choir, two hundred people changed their religion."* ~ **Fred Allen, ancient comedian who occasionally crossed swords with censors.**

In my relatively *(clearly debatable)* mature years, Denman has been an aural oasis for me. Shortly after deploying here permanently, I joined the peace choir. Unlike most of the choristers, I could not read music and was forced to actually remember tunes. My deficiencies, though obvious, were tolerated and, for a couple of years, I trilled with choral relish.

As I write this, the old peace choir may resurge. I belong to the Audio Arts Collective *(a tale I'll save for another day.)* Given the lack of harmony that infuses political life on Denman, the wise course for me would be for me to return to harmonic simplicity. Choirs demand an ability to compromise, to agree not only on the songs to be sung but in the singing of them. There is comfort in this. And limited collateral damage! Aside, perhaps, from tender eardrums!

Another Pointless Primer on Committee Protocol

"Outside of traffic, there is nothing that has held this country back as much as committees." ~ **Will Rogers.**

Committees can be labyrinthian. Each operates amid its own rendering of ritual, of control, of hierarchy. If you are ensnared in more than one committee, often the only common denominator is your perception. In small communities, especially where you might frequently sit on a number of committees, often with some of the same people, your ability to make a distinction between mandate, friendship and community expectation can become somewhat murky, a sometimes knotty overlap of community and personality that can leave a deposit of imprecision. (*And, incidentally, let's acknowledge that the opportunity to sit on as many committees as you have the doggedness for is unbridled in the Denman Kennel.*)

Your personal committee style may precede you. You might be viewed as an effective and innovative committee member, or a name-dropping status seeker, or, on rare and wholly unjustified occasions, a bit of a seat warmer. You may be one or all of these. Often it depends on what the committee is supposed to do or how desperate it is *(and, it should be noted, most Denman committees likely are drenched with desperation, a condition known as "sweat equity.")* In the beginning of a committee's initial existence, or during its annual rekindling, some effort should be spent wrangling it into a considered coherency. Each member may have a distorted perception of what the committee should and should not be doing. Finding a congruous compromise is essential. Calling it a compromise, however, may be controversial depending on how willing the group may be in accepting uncharted middle ground. *"If you want to kill any idea in the world, get a committee working on it."* ~ **Charles F. Kettering.**

Committees need a purpose. They should also possess 'common purpose', a 'common cause.' The death knell for many committees is 'cross purpose'. Reasonable people, brought together by a vague understanding of the rationale for a committee, need to determine their common purpose by establishing, or reaffirming, terms of reference, as well as relevant policies, what they are supposed to do, how decisions will be made, whom the spokesperson is and the like. These should evolve by discussion and debate. Every twist and turn should be documented. You may be in a heap of trouble if none of this is thrashed out and you simply move forward without checking your organizational GPS.

Down the road, if there is an accidental or intentional deviation from the understood accord, it is more than likely that someone is operating at 'cross purposes.' Why they would do this is grist for a whole other series of articles. Suffice it to say that in a small community, it is not unheard of for a number of folks to be unofficial spokespeople for their organization or committee, even when they are no longer in a decision-making role. This can become awkward. While most organizations and committees don't have any real authority, they do usually have some responsibility...for something, surely. They might, for instance, be the go-to group for a particularly fiery issue-for example, speeding traffic, public washrooms, coal mines or pottery factories. Whatever the issue is, an off-beam, poorly developed message may rankle if delivered in a less than coherent manner, by a less than representative spokesperson. *"Whiskey is carried into committee rooms in demijohns and carried out in demagogues."* **Mark Twain.**

Committees, therefore, ought to have wise leadership. Much is expected of Committee-Chairs. They are expected to be not unlike fathers who were once viewed by troglodytes, as the head of the family *(or, as mothers came to be viewed as women's emancipation took hold in the latter part of the 19th century, firm, all-knowing, confident and rational, transporting these assumed attributes to the table, a table some in-expert struggling fellow had no doubt set)*. Complicating this cursory contemplation on leadership, women in the throes of liberation were also expected to maintain virtues attributed to them

91

centuries earlier: compassionate, efficient, tolerant, deferent, able to milk cows, and, ultimately, chattel. With apologies for my metaphorical gender stereotyping, it was difficult in this era of bent genders to find anyone with the requisite cross-gender skill set, no matter how bogus they actually were.

At times, people on committees get their dander up over leadership. Some leaders overreach, embrace command with a fury that belies their position. This is touchy stuff. One wants go-getters, people who actually do something. They set the course for committee work. We all benefit from their generated energy. At the same time, leadership is a learned behaviour and should be exercised with humility and discretion.

A sketchy scan of the current leadership of a small selection of our Island organizations reveals, well, not much, really. One organization is now piloted by a retired zoo manager. We might all agree that he brings an abundance of skills easily transferable to our rather anarchically wild and woolly preserve. Another group is run by a retired businessman. Another, a genial former low-level union activist, another, a no nonsense systems analyst, yet another, a retired teacher. Each likely speaks a slightly different organizational language. Babel can easily win out under these conditions! *"If you see a snake, just kill it-don't appoint a committee on snakes."* **Ross Perot.**

While committees are sometimes conferred with magical virtues, at their core they are simply a partnership of people trying to get something done. What sometimes throws them off the rails is the complexity of the task at hand. Funding, Government, community expectations, gossipy antecedents, these and myriad other factors are stewish lumps that sometimes make a muddle out of the best of intentions. Our Island is a varicose vein-like schema of purplish people-eating committees. If someone spawns an idea to do one simple thing, the odds are a committee will be struck. Committees and sub-committees are struck, not unlike pedestrians are struck, sometimes even within the safety of a cross-walk. My point, you query? We have way too many committees, way too many organizations. And there is no end in sight. They all do valuable work, or might, someday. Winding down a committee or an organization is like severing a limb! Why would you do it? Especially if it does something worthwhile! Or used to! Or might, some day! There's no getting away from it, committees are a way of life hereabouts.

The Chicken Lady, the Dora, a Dash of Art and a Pint of Politics

"For those of us who can't quite forget Dora, there is still the sign outside the community hall saying "Dora Drinkwater Library". ~ **Extracted from the Small Talk column by Misinformation, the Flagstone, December, 2005**

I go to a lot of trouble to avoid work. Just ask my poor life partner. So when I was asked to consider writing an article about the Dora Drinkwater library, weaving in a narrative about Betty-Ann Grodecki *(Chicken Lady, Horsewoman, Librarian, Publisher, Impresario and Advocate to name a few of her personas,)* while quietly honouring Guenter Heim, the artist who painted the two delightful watercolours which now hang in the Library, paintings donated by Betty-Ann's children, and all of it intended to gently draw attention not only to the donated art pieces but also to hint at the need for a smidgen of unpretentious promotion for the somewhat under-utilized DD, I thought, I'm really not the best one for this. I have a track record of under-appreciating art, of failing to grok meaning. And I draw on cheap puns, lesser ideas, and pointless chatter to flesh out my articles. It just didn't seem right to ask me.

That aside, others, too few to name, massaged the situation and here I am. *"What was she thinking? Sooner or later she's going to have to be replaced."* **Misinfo talking about herself** *(and her suspicion that frère Jack's crucial editorial snippery might well spell the end of her gossip empire)* **in Small Talk, the Flagstone, September 2006.**

I don't believe Betty-Ann Grodecki will ever be replaced. None of us are,

93

really. Replaceable, that is. Some of us more, or less, of course, than others. In fact, in the few months after Betty-Ann died, some aspects of her definitely disappeared. Her buckshot-gun column, *Small Talk,* vapourized. Though likely welcomed by those few who never like to see their names and their social where-withals in print, the quality on occasion, and the quantity always of her tittle-tattle natter has gone to Boot Hill and I, for one, miss it. Her loving brother Jack Mounce, on the front page of the December, 2006 Flagstone illustrated her style of tell-tale writing by saying *"she wrote quickly, and had no time to check her facts......Some people were angered or hurt by her unintended inaccuracies, and she was always quick to offer retractions and abject apologies."*

The Sunday opening hours at the DD Library also went poof with Betty-Ann's departure. Though it was, on one level, a minor and necessary contraction in the hours of operation for the volunteer Library, staffed as it was at the time by a retinue of venerable elder women, it actually did denote a measurable lessening in service to the community. Her commitment to Sundays at the Dora was but one vivid example of her characteristically generous nature. ***"Perhaps no place in any community is so totally democratic as the town library. The only entrance requirement is interest."*** **Lady Bird Johnson.**

When I first settled on Denman, I looked around for things to do. While there were plenty of quaint and nifty endeavours one could sign up for, I was mesmerized by the Dora Drinkwater. More than just the books were the eclectic, eccentric collage of volunteers, led by Betty-Ann, Diane Davis and Wendy Reimer, who, collectively, seemed to rule the roost. I had an inkling, a peculiar one I confess, that the DD was the hub of the Island. All the important documents about land use and traffic were stored there in planned disarray. Humongous volumes of that Islands Trust Bible, the OCP *(which either stands for Official Community Plan, or Obsessive-Compulsive Plan depending on your druthers)* were also featured prominently. High on the history wall, volumes of old island publications, diaries, almost, of times past, clung together in dusty, crinkly unison. Surely here was the center of the Denman universe. As a rapidly aging, newbie male, I infiltrated a cosmos of thoughtful Island woman who carried on a respectful tradition of collecting, processing and signing out books for most anybody who wanted them. There were no fines, no punishment for tardiness in returning the books though, I have to say, there was a sly sense of vendetta whenever the since-lamented

Wall of Shame was salaciously referenced. *"Your Library is your portrait."* **Holbrook Jackson.**

The DD is no 'art' gallery. However, with the addition of the two Guenter Heim landscapes, it has significantly upped its ante. Guenter first came to Denman in the late 1970s and, as is the custom of some, visited at least once more some years later before acquiring land in 1986. Wikipedia, my latter-day impeccable source, describes him as *"a Canadian artist notable for his impressionistic landscapes of western Canada."* After working as a television artist and educator in Ontario, he moved to the province next door to us *(I don't have to name it, do I?)* in 1977. There, as the un-wikified thread declares, he worked *'in oil, acrylic and watercolour'* and his subjects included *'ranch, genre and prairie scenes near Edmonton and Calgary, Alberta and in the Okanagan, British Columbia.'*

The two paintings, recently mounted in the DD, quietly offer, in one, a bucolic view of Hornby, circa 1991, and in the other, undated, timeless, a subdued glimpse of a rural Denman. Initially a gift from the artist to his friends Betty-Ann and Wenzel Grodecki, they now look down from the wall behind the Librarians desk in the library that Betty-Ann loved so much. *"If truth is beauty, how come no one has their hair done in a library?"* **Lily Tomlin.**

I would not be surprised to stroll into the Dora one day and find someone having their hair done. I admit, as a marriage commissioner who happens to have access to the Dora, that I have used the space on infrequent occasion to meet budding brides and grooms. Not often, but when it seemed convenient. There, that's out! And what a huge relief! It's a useful place, the Dora, with a sort of rustic, multi-tasking disposition.

To wrap-up, someday, likely in the way distant future, especially given the economic barrel-scraping the Gordo-Liberals are mucking with, Denman may reclaim some of its tax dollars in the form of an actual branch of the Vancouver Island Regional Library. I strongly endorse this change. I hasten to add that Betty-Ann had her misgivings. But I also value, as I trust she did, the prodigious funkiness of the Dora. A graceful confederacy of Denman funk and VIRL vitality may well prove a truly appealing and arty endeavour. I can hardly wait.

"That's a Great Idea"

"I can't understand why people are frightened of new ideas. I'm frightened of old ones." ~ **John Cage.**

We all have them. Ideas! They keep bursting into our brain like Taser-bolts in a lightning storm. Most are there for a fraction of a nano-second and then are gone...purged...vaporized...vanished in the twinkling of an eye-dea...and why you ask? Because, I suspect, the world often can only handle just so many ideas at a time. *(Think about Palestine and Israel if you want to imagine how two competing concepts can fail to cozy up in the same space.)* I know I can only juggle a handful at any given moment, actually, usually only one at a time with perhaps a second idea warming up in the batting circle.

On a crisp fall morning not so long ago, whilst harvesting potatoes with a dozen and a half members of the Spuds Collective, *(Check out* **www.wearespuds.blogspot.com/** *to have a gander at the group)* I waxed on preposterously *(evidently blitzed with an uber-tuber high)* about the need for a clever composter to jettison inconvenient ideas at Buckley Bay rather than lugging them back to our Island paradise, already floundering under the yoke of surplus thought. My opinion was *(and here you be the judge as to whether I have too many foolish notions)* that if you live in a recalcitrant hamlet, you need to be hyper-vigilant about re-inventing the way things are done. While few would actually say *"That's a great idea but if I were you, I'd keep it to myself,"* my experience has been that things are being done in mostly one way *(or no way)* and the consensus is that they should continue to unfold accordingly. *(It doesn't matter what is being referred to, this principle of* *comfortable perfection remains sacrosanct.)* **"I had a great idea this morning, but I didn't like it."** **Samuel Goldwyn.**

The more ideas you generate the thornier your life can become, especially if you don't screen out troublesome constructs. If you are one of the blessed who has brainstorms, but is not driven to actualize them, then you are free to plan and think till the cows come home...unless your idea is to make sure the cows can't find their way home. If that's the case, you might be toying with Mother Nature and you'd better hold your horses...so to speak. *(I struggle to speak ruralese with facility.)*

If you just like to idly dream up aberrant thoughts, toss them back and forth like beanbags, and then stuff them in that storage box you use to hoard fanciful fabrications you never want to think outside of ever again, well, the Denman Thought Police will probably leave you alone. *"You can judge your age by the amount of pain you feel when you come in contact with a new idea."* **Pearl S. Buck.**

Okay, I admit there may not be such a thing as the Denman Thought Police. Up till now, anyways. It was just a wacky image I conjured to house a contemplation of the triffidian inclination towards things staying the same and how, anytime someone suggests they might be improved upon, well, all manner of meaningless mêlées bubble up, *'a bubbling crude',* to cite Flat and Scruggs' cunning, reverse-gentry jingle that prefaced every episode of **The Beverly Hillbillies** *(itself a masterful inspiration that was thankfully allowed to live and enhance popular culture forever.)*

In choir a few nights ago, we sang an old favourite, Building Bridges *(the Greenham Common version-not one of the countless similarly titled country twangers.)* The thrust of this touching refrain is that we should forge unity amongst adversaries who share common goals. Being a trifling philosopher, I suggested, tongue firmly tucked in jowled cheek, that you should never try to build bridges in the Islands Trust: shades of the living spectre of Pat McGeer. Though we continued to sing the song, I sensed *(born, no doubt, from the guilt all remorseful punsters can't quite scrape from their soles when they grasp they may have stepped in someone else's emotional droppings)* that I had spoken an ill-considered thought, and perhaps ruined a wonderful song for some. Or perhaps no one was paying attention. I get that a lot. *"Ideas are like rabbits. You get a couple, learn how to handle them, and pretty soon you have a dozen."* **John Steinbeck.**

The problem, as Steinbeck so succinctly states, is that ideas breed like...bunnies. And, like reproducing rabbits, they also need to be managed. Communicable ideas, like the most pernicious of diseases, need to be kept in their place, like a maximum-security idea hutch. Otherwise you risk pandemic. For example, consider the advent of the horse and buggy. It augured a brief age of comfort and convenience, replacing, or at least augmenting, the horse as a means of conveyance. Then, a most disturbing IDEA sputtered along: the automobile. We have been internally and externally combusting ever since.

"A nice man is a man of nasty ideas." Jonathan Swift (1667–1745).

My Gentrified Soul column was always meant to portray slight vignettes about my experiences with a relocated life, observations that pop into my head like...popcorn. Some of them just sit there, hard kernels going nowhere. Others snap, crackle and...re-populate. I have felt duty-bound to examine myself, sensing I may have been plopped into someone's dustbin of notions about who apprentice Denmanians the likes of me are, what values we carry in our satchels, what hideous changes we are going to wrought. So, may I humbly say that before I let any of my ideas wrought away, I hope to continue chatting about them every once in a while.

This is part and parcel of developing my unabashedly unhinged Gentry Code of Conduct...which may prove to be a perfectly awful idea. Who's to say, eh?

A Meditation on the Taking and Giving of Umbrage

"I have lost friends, some by death, others through sheer inability to cross the street." ~ **Virginia Woolf.**

Consider for a moment the morphology of the word, 'umbrage.' Does it not hint at pause, at reflection, hesitation even? Ummmmm, you say! Not that far from Ommmmm, perhaps? Ombrage might very well be a suitably new and innovative construct. In those spheres where we are obligated to 'Om and get it,' umbrage might be better consigned to the rumble seat. Welts of ill-feeling, if they still lingered, would be hummed or ummed or Ommed away. How hummingly divine that would be! *"If your great umbrage would care to meet my high dudgeon at 12 paces, I would be happy to entertain you at dawn."* ~ **Benedict Arnold.**

At the end of a recent meeting of everyone's favourite Resident's Association, an occasional sparring adversary approached me to point out the error of my spoken ways. Even though I habitually misspeak, I not only took umbrage at this rather self-evident observation but tinged my curt comeback with a button of sharp bilge, feeling justified, especially after he haughtily disparaged my lame attempt to repel his reproach when I claimed I was speaking humourously *(a chronic fallback position of mine.)*

I immediately regretted draping my sorry self in the rags of hubristic umbrage. Like most reasonably weathered adults, I have some experience with 'sucking it up' no matter what imperfection or slight has been offered. People of adequate breeding should always attempt to deflect criticism by, if not turning the other cheek, at least offering a less bumptious rebut.

My sense though is that the gauche way in which my acquaintance and I jousted *(and okay, I was gauche, he was positively elegant)* had little to do with my impetuous words of the evening but rather stemmed from a festering chain of implicit and explicit skirmishes we have been witness, *(and no doubt party)* to, these past few years. Indeed, the past few fractious months were but an effervescent outpouring which added another crusty layer to the 2008 Trust election crusade and intertwining events of yore. *"Where two discourse, if the one's anger rise, the man who lets the contest fall is wise."* **Euripides.**

Reflecting on my experiences with the taking and giving of umbrage over the years, I like to suppose that I have generally succeeded in avoiding most interpersonal conflict. Sadly, I have wretchedly failed to sidestep all of it. This is a huge regret for me, perfectionist that I am. It would be too much to expect that life was so smoothly-sailed that one would not a feather-ruffler be. Still, I often step back, seeking a less contradictory retort, resisting, though some might think not, excessively argumentative engagement. This is how I have viewed myself and any role I have played in the perpetuation of conflict around me. It is a comfortable position. Pew–like! It has allowed me to think well of myself, to puff up and spout, *"Wow, that's another dash of discord I have brilliantly evaded."*

But, if I'm moderately more incisive, I can effortlessly document quarrelsome patches in my life which I helped inflame. Families, for instance, are a breeding ground for humongous umbrage. Slights can quiver endlessly down through the years. And families stick with you, like mould on a chunk of cheese squirreled away at the back of the fridge.

I confess! I take positions. And though my opinions are usually adequately reasoned, on some I have wavered more than is seemly. For instance, I have convulsed over time on the question of capital punishment. Hang it, I just can't seem to make up my mind. And the Olympics! As I write this, anti-Olympic umbragers are marshalling their riled selves to serve up a meal or three of annoyance. In response, Canadian Border officials are weeding out those who offend their unaccountable de-selection process. I would expect no less from both sides. *"People who fly into a rage always make a bad landing."* **Will Rogers.**

I was told a story recently. A youth soccer game was underway. One team was shellacking the other. A parent of a player on the high scoring side was

vociferous that more goals be scored. Apparently, there was an understanding within the league that it was preferred form to lessen one's enthusiasm if your side was winning. A parent on the losing side crossed around and suggested to the voluble parent that he cool his jets *(or words to that effect.)* After some moments of distillation, the parent who had been braced, feeling aggrieved, crossed around and let his umbrage vent. Whilst these two gentlemen engaged in their grim badinage, the coach of the losing side injected his enthusiastic opinion into the fray. A small riot ensued. At last report, it had become a minor cause célèbre in the governing circle that circumscribes it.
Muppet Lore

> **Waldorf:** *"That Miss Piggy takes umbrage at the slightest annoyance."*
> **Statler:** *"I usually take aspirin. Maybe I'll take some umbrage."*

A question finally thwacks me in the keister. Can umbrage really ever be reconfigured? As much of a peacemaker as I think I am, I'm with old Muppet man, Statler. Take an aspirin! Get over it! It may just be that the human condition requires a steady amount of umbrage. At this moment in the curve of time, Canada is led by the grand guru of umbrage proponents, Stephen-give-no-quarter-Harper. There is no bridge wide enough to escape his pique. Parliaments are sacked! Spring Breaks are crushed! And this is just dreary old, self-absorbed Canada, a nothing-much-amiss Junior U.S. of A., you might say. What would our leader be like if we were a real country? Oops! Did I ruffle your patriotic plumage? All I was trying to do was plum the pitted depth that is umbrage.

A Smidgeon on Tradition

"Tradition is the illusion of permanence." ~ **Woody Allen**

On a wet warm winter day, whilst trying to dodge housework and other *domisilly* tasks, I began to give some thought to the age-old concept of 'tradition.' It came about after a nuptial reproach about personal responsibility. As a member of the occasionally maligned gentry *(OMG)* of Denman, I am, with the scurrilous solicitude of a morally ambiguous pundit, in the assumed position of observing, with a blasé lust for pointless improvement, the hold that tradition has on my adopted community.

Tradition, it seems to me, is the subjugation of the way it used to be on the way it seems to be now. Implicit in tradition is that it should always be the way it was. Of course, it never is, and the way the way it was is recalled is often at variance not only with the way it really was but muddying the memory of it all is the overcast observation that few of us can fully agree with anyone else as to what it actually was like, back then. The hold that tradition has on people and procedures cares hardly a whit with these equivocations. Tradition is the voice of the past even if that voice speaks in tongues. We are expected to show our respect for tradition by following its path, its precepts, its permanently unparalleled perfection, its choke-hold, or perhaps yoke-hold, *(or even, depending on your proclivity, toke-hold)* on every breath we consider taking. ***"Tradition means giving votes to the most obscure of all classes -- our ancestors. It is the democracy of the dead. Tradition refuses to submit to the small and arrogant oligarchy of those who merely happen to be walking around."* Gilbert K. Chesterton.**

Every organization, club, committee, even a friendship of two, is clad in the raiment of ritual. The garland of convention trickles out from the walls of musty museums, from shared obligations, from social comfort foods, grown, preserved or pickled. Tradition has many voices. Activist historians of the way it used to be are often quite adept at plucking past practice out of their pristine memory vaults and parading these feathered, occasionally innocently fabricated factoids, on to the stage of irrefutable folk-lore. Though risk of opposition always exists on these occasions, most of us cling tenaciously to our defective memory of the way things were, effectively boasting to whom we usually boast, that we are the sum total of our memories and experiences. Therefore, the only way we can truly know ourselves is to reaffirm ad nauseam how we came to this point in time. If we begin to doubt our recall of how we came to be, our sense of self becomes slightly unsteady. If on the other hand we persist in protecting our shape of memory, the contours of our collective life's traditions, we remain whole, unfettered, perhaps a mite shaken but absolutely, incontrovertibly unstirred... bonded, as it were, to our dusty martini lounge of memory, with or without olive. *"Almost every venerable tradition at a men's club starts out as a joke."* **Joe Bob Briggs.**

One night, decades ago, I was out on the town with a flock of friends. We were parched *(I had a substantial thirst back then.)* A beer parlour appeared on the horizon. It was a local Legion oasis. We attempted to affect entry. Nay, non-members, we were told, you may not enter. I explained that I had a few months of basic training under my belt. Though not a veteran, I had worn the uniform of my country, if ever so briefly. My comrades shied away. My truncated military experience was something I had rarely mentioned, especially in mixed counterculture company. My peacenik pals were amusingly appalled, but soberly tolerant. We trudged on, whistles left dry and unsaturated. Some weeks late, still niggled by memories of my unquenched ambition, I marched into the Legion in my home community. *"I'd like to sign up,"* I said. *"Fine. lad,"* they said. *"You need to be vouched for." "But I know no one here,"* I lamented. *"Not to worry, lad!"* With that reassurance, I was escorted downstairs to the Legion's cavernous tipple parlour. Four patrons were seated in a dimly-lit far corner. *"Gentlemen,"* the official said, *"Would two of you care to nominate this fellow for membership?"* In the hopped-up darkness, the old soldiers looked up, beer glasses clutched in hand, eyes misting, cheeks flush, and one said, *"Buy us a round, bucko and we'll nominate ye King."* With that endorsement, beer was replenished, forms filled out, including my military ID serial number which is burned into my brain to this day, and I became a latter-day Domestic Legionnaire. *"If at first you don't succeed, try again. Then quit. There's no use being a damn fool about it."* **W.C. Fields.**

After more than half dozen years on Denman Island, I have come to appreciate the intricacy of becoming involved and actually *wanting* to offer an innovative thought here and there. Not that I have had any meritorious notions that might upset susceptible Island apple carts. The unspoken expectation, that you blend in to whatever organization you join, accept the way things are done, be content to know that however things get done, that's probably the best way it could have been done, I have resolutely endorsed.

Of course, sometimes it's not the message but the messenger that offends the tribe. Most of us like to have a grasp of our community, who does what, who stands for what, and who gets things done. On a slow island, the ethos of the rest of the world, progress or bust, gets turned on its head. Visionaries are feted, not for looking into the future, but for training their ocular skills backwards. *"Tradition is a guide and not a jailer."* **Somerset Maugham.**

But back to the Legion that once took me in. Decades later, a Non-Profit Society I volunteered with *(and, subsequently, worked for)* bought that old Legion building. The Legion has long since left, having sold the structure to BC Transit. Located almost directly under pillars that carry Sky train, it was a timely investment. It is now the flagship for a multi-million-dollar social service agency. The Gym of the old building is a fully accredited independent school. And the beer parlour, well, independent schools are encouraged not to sell brew, no matter how income generating the activity might be. That dank old soldier's cellar, for a time an indoor archery range, is now a hub of offices and meeting rooms and an often frenetic free clinic.

Need defines how you use space. Public or near-public spaces require re-invention over time. The emergence of the new Gym in the recesses of the Seniors Activity Center is one contemporary example: the settling in for the long haul of our Clinic is another. Life and spaces, composed of ever-reconfiguring rituals, refugees, buildings, the Canadian Legion, dreamers of every age, even the irksome gentry: one and all seeking a new definition, desiring nothing more than to shape new traditions, to reanimate their heart, to ponder new thoughts, to regain any courage lost along the way.

Casual Cogitations From a Subdued Gentry-Guy

"Researchers have discovered that chocolate produces some of the same reactions in the brain as marijuana. The researchers also discovered other similarities between the two but can't remember what they are. " ~ **Matt Lauer**

In the social orbits I organically steer on Denman, (*I confess they are few and far between*), there is a deep-rooted understanding. Pot is grown in profusion on the Island. It's a given. Even if people don't actually have firsthand knowledge, they know it, like they know their name.

If nothing else, we grasp it because the RCMP Marijuana Air Force frequently buzzes overhead to scout out felonious foliage. Despite the fact that this admirable crime-fighting aerial *(and terrain-ical)* assiduity takes precious time away from much needed Taser excellence classes, one has to admire the zeal of these intrepid, hornswoggling, horticultural pursuits.

But, though a given, what impact pot-tery has on the economy of the island is a numerical enigma. And to talk about it, well, that's a trifle dodgy. So, I'm stopping here unless my moles care to raise my reservoir of knowledge. *"I'm frightened of eggs, worse than frightened, they revolt me. That white round thing without any holes... have you ever seen anything more revolting than an egg yolk breaking and spilling its yellow liquid? Blood is jolly, red. But egg yolk is yellow, revolting. I've never tasted it.* "**Alfred Hitchcock**

Shifting to the sticks, modifications have to be made. Your urban skills, those '*I lived in the city and knew what the devil I was doing'* methodologies, may not serve you well in your rustic refuge. Take egg acquisition. We're talking a lifetime of supermarket know-how, years of experience strolling the aisles, eggs piled dumpty over humpty, a limitless collection of cardboard-cosseted hen-spawn from chicken factories hither and yon are there for the picking. You can do it in your sleep! Simple! Straightforward! You don't have to scramble from pillar to post to find an egg to crack.

On Denman, a more modestly enticing, though by no means unique, marketing scheme exists. While eggs are expediently available at the revered General Store *(for those slowly inching themselves into Ruraltania)* a host of independent egg producers hawk their wares by the side of the road. You and your latent omelette-chery inclinations are hailed over by the most unambiguous of advertising. EGGS!!! Drop what you're doing. Pull to the curb! And, in honour box tradition, leave the requested coin in the coffer. *"Advice is seldom welcome, and those who need it the most, like it the least."* **Lord Chesterfield**

It is a certainty that newbies will *(and should)* ask questions. It's in their nature. They want to know how the lay of the land...got laid. Why are things done the way they are? How are they done? Who can tell me why? For example, why are there so many committees on Denman? Why are there so many community buildings? Why are some tax supported and some not so much or not at all? Some of these community *(or quasi-community)* facilities are: The Old School *(Islands Trust begat by DIRA);* The Arts Centre *(just begat);* The Fire Hall *(The Regional District doesn't begat anything);* The Seniors Hall *(its begating days quite possibly may be rising again)*; The Community School *(The School District awkwardly begets itself...a not unpleasant experience I'm told);* The Community Hall *(Begat by all of us and by no one...an orphan begat.)*

What business of mine should I mind and what questions are up for grabs? *"Jerry Ford is a nice guy, but he played too much football with his helmet off."* **Lyndon B. Johnson**

Ah, the helmet issue. Well, with me, it's more a tremendous trepidation. Although it has been some time since I have felt the inclination to observe bicycle behaviour in the big city, I believe urban bikers have, for the most part, adapted quite nicely to the mandatory wearing of helmets. It helps to have cops and cameras on every corner. While a few rogue riders still pedal their unprotected wares, most city denizens reason that metropolitan living is so perilous that only someone content to get by on their personal charm would take unnecessary chances with their noggin. Rural life is a lot less dicey, unless you're like me and have been bumping your head against various walls and ceilings for years.

Our roads are bucolic little passageways, safe for ambling, for peddling, for horsing about. Drivers, in the main, are respectful. They don't want to run people off the road. I'm sure of that. Except when they turn ferry-feral! Although being in a hurry is actively discouraged on Denman, there is very little that can be done with those who are stricken with a ferocious case of ferry-ferality. They are hell-bent for Hornby or Buckley Bay and the devil take those who impede them, helmet or bare-headed.

"After enlightenment, the laundry." **Zen Proverb.** I've just finished a load of laundry. I like doing laundry. It has always been a task I could do well, on time and under budget. If there is a drawback to doing laundry at home, it's waiting for the inevitable meltdown of the appliances. The tension is a killer.

Some islands provide laundry service: Pender, Quadra, Gabriola are examples. Salt Spring Island, in a wink and a nod to women's liberation, once had Mrs. Clean Laundry. What an Island! It may no longer be in business. Never-you-mind-dearie, there are at least two other sources of clean and wholesome sheets on SS Isle.

On Denman, there is no public laundromat. I have no idea if there are plans for one. I wonder how you would go about developing a business plan for such an enterprise. Key to such an endeavor, no doubt, would be establishing a market. The question then arises: how would you determine the need. Does Stats Canada actually know how many washers and dryers there are on Denman? If they don't, what's wrong with the tools they use for the census? I'd be happy to say I have one of each. Nobody has ever asked. *"It's easy enough to read the thoughts of a newcomer. Everything seems beautiful because you don't understand."* **I Walked with a Zombie (1943)**

That's the beauty of culture shock! You take it a step at a time. Newcomer rural citizens begin to access gentry-level positions in the community. Volunteers are always needed. Slowly, they are trained in the mores of the community. After a suitable period of orientation, of coddling, they are vetted and, like cream, rise.

Bench Marks

"There was a long weathered carpenter's bench under the tall tree in front of the little old house that Lawrence had lived in there. I often lay on that bench looking up into the tree... past the trunk and up into the branches. It was particularly fine at night with the stars above the tree." ~ **Georgia O'Keeffe**

It was the last day of winter: a winter at once more gentle then we might have imagined but also a winter of hearty Olympian endeavours, of indiscriminate political embarrassments and of arbitrary, avalanching deaths. Having intentionally trimmed down my to-do list, and, sadly, giving little thought to the fate of podium people or rampaging snowmobilers cavalierly ripping into distant and dangerous mountains, I ventured into our little village to post a parcel and gather up stray gossip. The air was crisp. A streamer of wood stove smoke clung to the sky as I passed underneath. It dreamily drifted into a nearby meadow, thinning   into grey strips of smoky thread.

Our little Postal emporium these days is on the eastern end of a small lane and parking lot, a few meters from the rustic propane repository. The Post Office has a facade not unlike a passé Route 66 auto court, notwithstanding that it offers no overnight respite to transient travelers. Two ambitious apple trees, one on either side of its entrance, stand sentinel. One tree is bastioned in a patch of lawn. A rough-hewn bench rests along the grassy square, almost beckoning pooped parcel posters to take a pause before traipsing off into other demands of the day. Opposite it, facing the pot-holed parking lot, the second tree shadows a more delicate driftwood bench which eyeballs approaching traffic.

I post my package. Conversation is abetted by my aside that one of the benches has recently been repositioned. I am told it was done a while ago. I hadn't noticed. I tend to not notice the world in winter. Spring sparks my powers of observation. I step out into the open air. My mind ignites. Benches!!! Benches!!! *"The true morning sun, beaming through a half-closed window-shutter, fell upon a part of a bench ill-joined to a cottage-door;"* **Goethe**

A rudimentary mental ramble catches fire on this chilly sunny morn. Our downtown core is cleaved by two key island roadways. The sense is one of artless partition, a division born of time, human constraint and, perchance, a demitasse of planning. Perhaps there was a plan once upon a time, one that slowly coalesced as the motorway took shape, one of its era, one that suited the people of the day. As I plunk myself down on the post office bench, I contemplate the initial engineering. It must have been a deer trail, a cow path, a slug slide. I try to visualize other options. No luck. I am a creature of few designing insights.

The existing road doesn't really fetter safe foot travel, except for the less fleet-footed *(statistically a mushrooming number)* but the aesthetic is disconcerting. On busy days, thankfully few and far between unless you're a merchant, there is some risk as stretched trucks with long decks stick out their extreme bumptitiousness well into the roadway. Most drivers typically drive front end in, compelling the struggle later to back out into oncoming traffic. As the population ages, necks turn with less fluidity: need for caution heightens, ability lessens. *"I really believe I was happier when I slept on a park bench in Central Park than during all the years of the 'perfect lover' stuff."* **Rudolph Valentino**

The very best benches sit in simple yet elegant settings, classic nooks under speckled Arbutus or lofty Oak, rocky knolls reaching out into a somnolent sea, soft paths winding throughout a churchyard. Some of these charming places of rest appear in surprising fashion. Occasionally, for example, as you stroll in some slightly pampered wood you may encounter one, placed by some parks worker, conservancy volunteer or trickster troll, each having brilliantly determined where you might need to unencumber yourself. *"A throne is only a bench covered with velvet."* **Napoleon Bonaparte**

In our village, paths wander through the underbrush. Short-cuts abound. Trails weave through the bramble, small bridges ford creeks *(except, for a time, the ancient Arts Centre bridge, washed away perhaps or collapsed from damp-rot and since rebuilt.)*

On a sunny Saturday recently, as hundreds of Islanders were gathering in the Community Hall to say farewell to a beloved Islander, I found myself, after exiting the Hardware store, paying unanticipated attention to our little Anglican Church, remembering I had, to that point, avoided roving its perimeter.

Seeking something akin to solace I found the shady grove wedded next to the little church. In the far corner, etched by peaceful paths, a memorial bench waits for the fatigued trekker. I spent a moment. Rested, I ventured around the front of the little church. Across the way, I spotted a glorious octagonal table-bench which has recently appeared in the front yard of *ye old Arts Centre*. It begs a roundtable discussion or a riotous game of outdoor Rummoli.

Thoughts less tangled, I sauntered up to the hall to say goodbye. ***"Sometimes you get a glimpse of a semicolon coming, a few lines farther on, and it is like climbing a steep path through woods and seeing a wooden bench just at a bend in the road ahead, a place where you can expect to sit for a moment, catching your breath"*** **Lewis Thomas.**

The 1941 Raoul Walsh classic, High Sierra, kick-starts with Bogart's character, Roy Earle, being sprung from the Indiana State Pen after an eight-year stretch. The first thing he does is go to a nearby park to sit on a beautiful bench, resting under a shedding Maple tree. He just wants *"to make sure that the grass is still green and the trees are still growing."* It is, and they are. Still, the world has changed for his character.

Bogart's brief reflection is one of my favourite moments in film. For Roy Earle, for anyone seeking a toddy of tranquility, all they have to do is wander to a bench and plop down for a while. For Island dwellers, beach and bench and reach of sea are part of our spirit. And once you start finding benches, for they are in the most unexpected places, set awhile and reaffirm that *"the grass is still green and the trees are still growing."*

Small Corruptions

"I don't make jokes. I just watch the government and report the facts." ~ **Will Rogers**

Not so long ago, in the squirrely way events unfold in the sandbox that is our Nation's Capital, Federal politicians stood up *(to a man and woman)* and blocked the Auditors General's attempt to review their personal allowance spending. Each MP gets at least $400,000 to run their offices, fly to wherever, take family members occasionally along: perks, they are, small little taxpayer funded pleasures.

I was taken aback by this blatant demonstration of ...what? What exactly was it that drove these representatives of the public weal to defend their inalienable right not to cough up evidence that would either counteract or confirm concerns about their clearly-presumed-to-exist excesses? It was only a few short months earlier that we had learned about the exploitation of political allowances by the vacuous representatives of the painstakingly distorted British political system. I am still lurching from the news that one entitled fellow, Conservative Cabinet Minister Douglas Hogg, aka Viscount Hailsham *(burdened forever with the linguistic extract both of hog and sham,)*, used public monies to have his moat cleared. *(Moats do plug up apparently, somewhat, I imagine, like septic systems.)*

British Columbia also has a significant contingent of elected representatives who are antsy about disclosing how they spend discretionary funds. Against a backdrop of unparalleled leadership adjustment, this alarm about small corruption has fallen, temporarily, by the wayside. *"Corruption is nature's way of restoring our faith in democracy."* ~ **Peter Ustinov**

Most of us don't have to face a giant public eye watching our small missteps and petty vices. Occasionally, in an era increasingly prone to spotlight, flash-in-the-pan, fifteen minute personalities, poor, ambitious, incautious souls are caught up in some seedy scandal or abuse of their nine hundred seconds of fame. Inelegantly propelled into the limelight, their previous lives have ill-prepared them for the obfuscation, secrecy and viscosity required to manage the grotesque glare. And they are given precious little time to develop a thick skin or embrace the temperate-seeming behaviour required to have some longevity amongst the notorious. Some propelled into warts-and-all prominence do survive quite nicely with most of their values and personal equilibrium intact. The customary understanding of how they manage this mission is that they *'keep true to themselves.'* Depending on the venue, this is not easily managed.

Surely everyone wants to *'keep true.'* Those who are most able to achieve this ethical nirvana are likely the most isolated of hermits. They have simplified their world to the bone, pared it down to a straight line from which they never deviate. They do not yearn for public office, nor, for that matter, seek the company of others. They exist in a cone of unremitting minimalism. Monk-like, nothing can intrude on their perfection, least of all the inescapable corruption found in human company. ***"The most practical kind of politics is the politics of decency."*** ~ **Theodore Roosevelt**

But we are not wired to be a world of isolates. Humans are social creatures. We are compelled to seek ways to engage, ways of maintaining the world within an intense yet orderly prism. We seek compromise. Bismarck correctly opined that *"politics is the art of the possible."* Most reasonable decisions seek a broader reach, a more universal buy-in. They have a tinge of conciliation about them. On the other hand, we often are not privy to the hard-tack, give and take we might imagine occurs in smoke-filled backrooms. The recent announcement by Premier Gordon Campbell that he was resigning, a most reasonable decision you would have to say, engendered a host of unpleasant observations and verbal back-flips of joy. My political party of choice, in an overly-exuberant expression of unpleasantness, sent out an e-missile suggesting we all have a party. In short order, the smug NDP found itself in the midst of its own irreversible squabble. Though it may not have acquired the cachet of 'the Night of the Long Knives' – the Nazi's unfortunately continue to offer up horribly exaggerated metaphors for lesser political skullduggery – one might consider calling this abrasively self-destructive NDP hiccup 'The Night of the Long Nails.' That is, one might if one had irresistibly poor judgement!

Somewhere along the way, kindness and decency have been traded in for partisanship, crudity and, for my complicit part, irony, satire and cheap jokes. While the world stage is rife with examples, the unctuous truth is that most of us revel in this practice. There is a need to poke a little fun at somber engagement. Laughter, in moderation, keeps us all honest...and entertained. *"I never vote for anyone. I always vote against."* ~ **W.C. Fields**

Notwithstanding seasonal goodwill, there is the smoke of survival and intemperate discord in the air, not just on Denman but around the world. Classic opponents face off as their parents did, as their grandparents did. Masses of humanity, immigrants, refugees, travelers of all descriptions are moving in waves, clusters of the exiled seeking the solace and security of a forgiving sanctuary. Even in the wake of the recent horrific catastrophe on Christmas Island–migrants seeking a promised land and many swallowed up in the turbulent sea–some federal politicians here exhibited a fondness for exposing their cherished agenda against human smugglers.

We are led to believe that the seas are swollen with pirates and scallywags poised to jump ship and pummel our peace and prosperity. On the high seas, human smugglers transport their desperate passengers. On Denman, mercenary travel agents are afforded a similar characterization. As ever, the comfortable applaud extremism in the defense of THEIR liberty. That's the ticket! *"If you could kick the person in the pants responsible for most of your trouble, you wouldn't sit for a month."* ~ **Theodore Roosevelt**

Who is responsible if the world isn't as perfect as we imagine it should be? Surely someone must be? However, once one leaves the womb, or at least the familial cudgel, we have to accept our own contribution to how the world is, its impact on us, and our response to it. Yes, there are larger forces at play that descend on us with blunt force: political upheaval, nature run amok, the Almighty *(or his buck)*. But eventually it is left to each one of us to stand up *(or down)* and stake out our position. How we manage the everyday small corruptions that tempt us is probably the greatest measure of who we are. How these small corruptions insinuate themselves into our everyday lives, how we choose to influence *(or be influenced by)* those within our crop circle, speaks volumes about what sort of world we desire.

Conversation Stoppers and Other Bungles

"The difficulty with this conversation is that it's very different from most of the ones I've had of late. Which, as I explained, have mostly been with trees."
~ **Douglas Adams**

You can often tell when a conversation should not have been initiated. That flash of insight abruptly arrives when someone storms out of the room or when the phone is slammed down. Those remaining in the room, suddenly swept up in the backwash of a hasty departure, are left with little recourse. Many times it is considered unseemly to even acknowledge the irretrievable exit. If some sort of formal meeting is underway, invariably someone picks up a safe thread and people just move on. Some may want to express concern for the dearly departed, may even offer a hapless homily to capture the feeling of fretfulness that clings to the room like shards of pastry dripping from a pizza parlour ceiling.

By the same token, once a phone receiver is slammed down on the cradle, by you or the party on the other end, *(and here I recognize some younger people may be unfamiliar with this obsolete means of disconnecting)* the person hung up on is left in a taciturn lurch.

Complicating these two typical venues of communication is the volatile specter of e-mail. HAVE YOU EVER RECEIVED ONE OF THOSE EMPHATIC E-MAILS WHERE EVERY WORD IS CAPITALIZED? You can see and hear the end of any civil dialogue in the mere presentation of such angry emphasis. If you do receive such a communiqué, you can be sure that conversation has ground to a halt before you reload and fire a pointlessly petty return salvo. *"Drawing on my fine command of language, I said nothing."*
~ **Robert Benchley**

I recently attended the wake of a long-time acquaintance. I hadn't seen him in years. I struggled to remember any specific repartee he and I may have had. None jumped to the fore. Yet, when we saw each other, we would banter and commingle in tiny yet consequential ways because of our shared experiences. I was once known to natter a lot. He was a quiet fellow. As I sat in his brother's spacious backyard and heard chunks of his life remembered in choked up and caring tones, I wondered at my failure to have pivotal tête-à-têtes with any number of other people in my life. By the same token, I wondered at some of the less successful discussions I may have had with people who simply weren't interested in me or my thoughts.

At the wake, another comrade recalled a display of mine back in the mid-sixties. I was an undergraduate at SFU. Two accomplices and I determined that a certain Prof was a bit of a hypocrite. Years before I understood and appreciated my own beguiling duplicity, we three decided to parse the Profs personality into three portions. One fine day we commandeered his lecture hall and proceeded to expose his three pretentious personas. Apparently we stood on desks and perpetrated vociferous blather to grind out our prodigious thrust.

Universities should encourage these sorts of self-expression. We got to act like smug bores; he, perhaps, wrote an article and enhanced his Curriculum Vitae. *"The real art of conversation is not only to say the right thing at the right place but to leave unsaid the wrong thing at the tempting moment."*
~ **Dorothy Nevill**

A short time ago a letter I submitted to the local press was printed. Some days later, an acquaintance sent me a long rebuke. His letter of reproach said, in part, that *"I fear that the tone and content of your letter helps enforce the perception that we Islanders are prone to whining and a sense of entitlement."*

As you may deduce, we are both Islanders he and I. Well, he is a long-time Islander and I am a relative newcomer. He lives on an Island well known for being a contented Isle. Mine is legendary for being cranky. Neither observation is necessarily true. Still, both are probably closer to the mark than either of us might care to admit.

The word *'conversation'* has always struck me as inherently negative. I'm more in favour of *'pro-versations'*. Still, no matter my little creative spin, pro or conversation between those with different styles can be awkward. And we all have little boundaries, things not to be said, gestures controlled, verboten territory. This very article, a bit of a one-sided conversation at best, should probably have been more prudently considered. Alas, I often succumb to temptation. *"It was impossible to get a conversation going; everybody was talking too much."* ~ **Yogi Berra.**

I strive to be pithy. My paramount principle, as both ponderer and essayist, is to sum up complex and diverse notions in snappy little capsules. Pithy plucky epithets! My life's goal! Frequently, away from my word processor, important concepts get lost in my loose undisciplined ravings. In a dialogue duel, pithiness easily escapes me. I drone on. I want to clarify my every stray subtle distinction. Conversations under my tutelage often achieve nothing other than to worsen an already strained situation.

In the past few years, I have taken up the pen with a rampaging waterway of whimsical riposte. I have mostly swapped my spoken sword's dull blade in favour of obscure observation, fine-tuned with trivial garnish, broken twigs of parsley-weight prose.

For those with a soberer bent, I am a lowly pimple, more zit than wit. I have come to accept this appellation. I find chaotic, ironic digression much more rewarding than speechifying. *"I often quote myself. It adds spice to my conversation."* ~ **George Bernard Shaw**

Sometimes I enhance my scribbled observations with excessive narrative, wandering all over the dust-dry desert in search of some thoughtful oasis. There is always material. As I conclude this middling meditation, I lament all the frank conversations with friends and foes that will not find voice. I am even loath to have forthright discussions with myself for fear I might say something disagreeable. Or worse, I might hear something in my tone of voice that requires immediate reparation. Hampered by my own inability to have a civil let alone substantial discussion with myself how can anyone expect me to have a crucial chinwag with them? That's just asking too much.

More Casual Cogitations From a Cowed Gentry-Guy

"Every crowd has a silver lining" ~ **P. T. Barnum**

One of the tremendous delights about summer on the Island is the availability of garden-fresh vegetables. A significant residual benefit for me of these greens *(and yellows, oranges, purples and reds as well)* is the capacity to stay on the Island, occasionally drift down to the Saturday Market, General Store as of late, or the open-daily Summer produce shack, and replenish. That's my perspective. But for the occasionally beleaguered farm merchant, and I'm thinking here of Patricia Piercy and her cozy little combo veggie produce hut and reading room, a long weekend swarm of veggie hunters could be a claustrophobia-inducing nightmare. Crowds of tens swarming like...all those creatures that swarm. Bees! Wasps! Tourists!

One doesn't often encounter a clustering of humanity on Denman. When it does occur, it can be an unsettling experience, enough to drive even the most garrulous chatterbox to hide in their cellar until things thin out or some semblance of pastoral equilibrium is found.

Two Septembers ago, the Grapevine announced that the produce shack, Patricia and Wes Piercy's essential outpost, would be 'under new management.' This seamless transfer from one generation of produce-farmers to the next goes against the trend. However, it has proven a positive change.

Except the crowds seem to have increased due in large part to the Chuck Wagon Burger emporium that is quickly becoming the summer go-to place. *"I live in a high rise with my family part of the year in New York and I don't know three quarters of the people in the building. We live in the same square-footage and I wouldn't know who they were".* ~ **Dan Aykroyd**

Not so long ago, a newspaper carried the following headline: 1,700 left homeless by massive Toronto fire. The thirty-story building, with 711 living units was struck by a blaze on the 24th floor. No one died. A thought *(admittedly a less than novel notion)* was born from news of that conflagration. That one building housed almost double the population of Denman. Yet, proximity does not necessarily promote intimacy or awareness. By the same token, Denman, though in many ways a hot bed of intimate relations, *(certainly the tenor of historical reportage if not latter day gossip,)* is also a disparate world with a dispersed population. We are likely heading towards the state of affairs experienced by Hornby, where upwards of sixty percent of the housing is owned by those who live elsewhere much of the year.

Though one would be hard-pressed to condemn this state of affairs, *(one could, I suppose, but who would listen.... those left behind to manage the community or those who require two or more abodes to house their ambitions,)* it is an unsettling condition. ***"Whenever I was upset by something in the papers, Jack always told me to be more tolerant, like a horse flicking away flies in the summer."*** ~ **Jackie Kennedy**

In the Men's Stall at the Denman West Ferry Terminal, the corpses of last summer's flies, trapped in a neon coffin-cage, clung together in each other's company, high above the intimate activities of humans. They were decomposing there for months. Possibly years! I should have been paying more attention. In any case, there were in the vicinity of forty or fifty of the fly cadavers, sticking to the ceiling like dark freckles. For a time, there were also wads of toilet paper, spit-ball shaped, peppered into the ceiling as if shot from a shotgun. Sometime around summer's dawn, they were whisked away.

Recently, I had cause to visit the Denman West Loo again. I was pleased to note that, like the swallows of Capistrano, the dead flies of Denman have begun to return. My need for order has yet again been met. ***"I believe in opening mail once a month, whether it needs it or not."*** ~ **Bob Considine.**

Transmitting communication on Denman takes a variety of forms. Aside from the traditional means, snail mail *(perhaps it should be called slug mail on Denman,)* e-mail for those with the courage to use it, Mr. Bell's brilliant device, as well as a classic hoot and a holler, we are also blessed with the iconic Denman Free Post. Located in Abraxas, it has operated as a crucial repository for intra-Island transmissions to anyone familiar with both the alphabet and clutter, for upwards of fifteen years. It is a marvelous service, a sort of stationary go-between for all sorts of packages, letters, and bric-a-brac. There is absolutely no cost.

But it does have its downside. No one manages it. Freepost depends on the kindness, the promptness of all the friends and strangers who use it. A letter or package left should be picked up as promptly as a Denmanian can muster. So, you see the problem. Some letters of the alphabet are much more in demand. Given that most organizations on Denman begin with the letter D, D is inundated. As are C and B, to name but a busy few.

Apparently, on rare occasions, those whose letter of the alphabet has a higher demand and a perennially more desperate need for pruning to find salvation, drive some, out of shear desperation, to go free postal. Phone calls are made. Tardy, sometimes forgetful, addressees are urged to unclog the free postal conduit. No one wants that call. Pick up your mail, your free mail.

"If motherhood doesn't interest you, don't do it. It didn't interest me, so I didn't do it." ~ **Katherine Hepburn.** Though I personally wonder what sort offspring might have sprung from the theatrical womb of the great Hepburn, she did do her bit to assist the world to not reach seven billion any sooner than it did, which, incidentally, befell us on All-Hallows' Eve 2011...less of a treat and hardly a trick, really.

Denman seems to be doing its part as well, a la the great Hepburn. The latest Census 2011 stats show that our population has declined from 1095 in 2006 to 1022 last year. This represents a decline of 6.7 % against a net increase in BC of 7%. Many Islands in the Trust have suffered *(or benefitted, depending on your persuasion)* from this population implosion. Hornby is down a frightening 10.8 percent. By contrast, Lasqueti is up by a magnificent 18.7 percent.

In May, we'll know the demographic breakdown. That will tell us whether we are bearing more children than before or whether my demographic, the noxious baby-boomer, is skewing the stats. Whatever the age, we are in a deficit. I think that's a problem.

Recluses, Hermits, Writers and the Community

"The writer is either a practicing recluse or a delinquent, guilt-ridden one; or both. Usually both." ~ Susan Sontag.

I have been waiting for a dose of inspiration for a quite some time now. I fret that the longer it takes to arrive, the less likely I will recognize it when, or if, my modest muse should put in an appearance. Much of my life has been full of these dawdling inspirational moments...moments foolishly withered in expecting strikes of inspired lightning: In frustration, these brain flashes likely go elsewhere seeking a more receptive audience.

As a result, I often feel the complete dullard. All around me, material percolates. Conversations go on about the most amazingly everyday (*I had planned to use 'mundane' but thought better of it*) subjects. Grandchildren! Fish! The Economy! Coal Mines! And, time and again, what mostly preoccupies many of the denizens of Denmanistan...Art. Our Island, much like other water-logged entities, seems to produce a huge swack of artists including painters, sculptors, potters, photographers, musicians, and, of course, writers! Galleries and Studios abound. Creativity coalesces like summer flies on roadside horse droppings...albeit year round. Yet, of all the imaginative arts, perhaps it is the poor, lower ranked writers (*I am a lifetime member*), those of us who burrow into our humble, emotionally cluttered root cellars to peck out our mysterious products, whom most often become recluses. As we puckishly hunker down in our creative lairs, every Tom, Dick or *Harried* visual artist can produce product at the drop of a barely heard hatpin, hold a show and allow the world to see their work. Written works are not so accessible. Voice, intonation, silent reading, there are so many aspects of the printed word; our art has innumerable nuances. Visual art is exactly what it seems, or what is read into it. Written Art is a puff of breath; if read by the recipient, it is as if life were pumped into the words; if read silently, dreams emerge. But who knows? How is this ecstasy shared? *"There is no way that writers can be tamed and rendered civilized or even cured. The only solution known to science is to provide the patient with an isolation room, where he can endure the acute stages in private and where food can be poked in to him with a stick."* ~ **Robert A. Heinlein**

I have long defined myself as a writer. In my earliest years, before I could actually print my name, this was clearly presumptuous. My first effort to share written work with an audience larger than my immediate family was an entry to the Vancouver Sun, to a sort of junior journalism contest. I was awarded an honourable mention for writing about a Legion branch in Burlen, Washington which was sending care packages to Berlin, Germany, at the time, *Commie* country. The crux of my article, aside from how similar the respective cities names sounded, was that hungry people were hungry people, no matter the redness of their politics. Unfortunately, there was no Burlen, Washington. The paper had mistyped Burien. Much of my article referenced the mistaken namesake cities and brotherhood. At least American Veterans feeding godless Marxists was not the error, though it was the issue.

If nothing else, this was a great beginning for one eventually devoted to writing about nothing in particular. The lesson learned: no one really cared what you wrote. Now that may have been a faulty assumption as clearly many people these days do care about what is written. And what is written is legion.

For the past couple of years, I have had a glorious writing chamber, a den, a writing womb where I plunk away on my word processor. I repair to this lair of sometimes limited literacy to osterize my increasingly geriatric creative fluids. Alone with my thoughts, they often feel abandoned. Still, in partnership, we persevere. *"Solitude vivifies; isolation kills."* ~ **Joseph Roux**

Two thirds of the way through this meditation *(a reflective and highbrow term I use for my prattle)* I am already way off my intentional mark. I had intended that this piece address an observation I had some time ago that the more artists you have in a community, the less politically engaged the citizenry are. If true, *(not a situation I often find with my observations,)* why would that be, I wondered? Art demands sacrifice. To economically or artistically survive as an artist, one has to block out the external world, be selective at the very least. What is often forfeited is time. Artists have to create. Artists have to employ business methods. Democratic engagement requires time and participation. Or so I was thinking. I rarely see artists at community meetings. Oh, sure, there are some who high step out, multi-tasking utopians for the most part, who can never decide what not to do. But the authentic artists, the ones who are obsessed with their creativity, consumed by a creative passion that demands total obedience, well, my impression is that they have no time for the jerkily inefficient dance of democracy, a dance which often sees the dancers stepping on toes, theirs and others; in lockstep, it can become some ungainly square dance in the round. *"A hermit is simply a person to whom civilization has failed to adjust itself."* ~ **Will Cuppy.**

A great deal of my life was spent in a vibrant urban setting. I resided in the Lower Mainland for most of the period 1965-2003. Almost forty years of alienating, exciting city life. I had acclimatized to the ways of pavement and concrete. Since exercising my right to downsize, little has changed. I confess to having the same, or similar, profligate pursuits as finagled many of my preoccupied city days. Excluding regular employment that is, as well as my modest domestic duties, I easily fell into many of those deceptively easy distractions any great conglomerated urban sprawl had to offer. Here, I am stymied only by my limited, slightly consumptive ambition.

There are two things I cannot imagine abandoning; writing and politically engaged community involvement. I need both. I thrive on both...even though I nurture my inner hermit with calorific food and aimless diversion. I find that often, each, writing and community involvement, blends, one into the other. One pulls me out of myself; the other draws me in to my core. Healthy tension to be sure, tension that is the sap of life; it either refreshes you or knocks you silly.

Classic Cinema Comfort Food

Helen: *I'm going to give you a piece of my mind...*
Francey: *Oh, I couldn't take the last piece.* **Vivacious Lady (1938) dialogue**

I started to write this slight meditation on my puzzling passion for old films in late winter. In almost spectral style, I have been showing classic films on Denman for four years. When I began, I had thought to show nothing but film noir: you know, dark urban mysteries, black and white manifestations, the type of film that these days sends conventional people running to the hills. My inaugural film, in late September 2007, was Jules Dassin's **The Naked City**. I chose it not only because it is a reasonably well known title *(and had spawned a TV series in the late 1950's a decade after the film premiered)* but also because New York struck me as the antithesis of the village of Denman.

Occasionally I still do show these menacing cinematic urban romps which are, as a rule, set in cold, pitiless, asphalt terrain. More and more however, I've tried to present classic comedy and drama, films with a broader sweep. I have shown at least twelve films from the American Film Institute's latest list of the 100 all-time classics. At a minimum, I now try to show at least twenty to thirty films a year. My routine, barring weather or inclement human episodes, is to show films starting in February and wrapping up by the end of June. In September, I resume the showings and conclude mid-November. *"For me, the cinema is not a slice of life, but a piece of cake."* ~ **Alfred Hitchcock**

What is it about old movies that lure us in? Many of us, at least those of a certain age, are simply familiar with them, some of them anyway. My generation in particular has had the ability to watch movies at will for decades. Early television presented a historically novel opportunity to survey a wealth of old films, many no longer in circulation. Growing up in the early 60's, one of my favourite shows was called British Sunday Theatre. Even though the fare was strictly old British flicks, it was a good education in film watching. A few years later, CBC presented many risqué French films late at night on weekends. For a time, at least until the censor woke up, these mostly Brigitte Bardot films provided me with an unexpected education in film appreciation. *"That's what I like about film-it can be bizarre, classic, normal, romantic. Cinema is to me the most versatile thing."* ~ **Catherine Deneuve**

Once in a while I decide to show a film that I haven't seen before other than when I preview it. (By the time I do present a film, I have previewed it, primarily for the quality of the tape or DVD, but also to reassure myself that it is as good as I remember it, that others will find some pleasure in it. Even with this preparation, I have had a few gaffs.) All in all though, I have met few films I didn't like. Many are like old friends, cinematic comfort food.

A recent film, **Mystery Street**, was appreciated by one cinema patron because the tale was comfortably linear. It began 'six months earlier' and moved ahead in a straightforward fashion. I knew exactly what he meant. Our own lives move forward in a step-by-step motion. If we, perchance, get knocked off our path, we get confused, out of sorts, at loose ends in the bramble. Hopefully we can re-orient ourselves and continue in a relatively straight forward motion.

Life's inauspicious roadblocks pester us constantly. Parents of younger children and those folks and others who are busy with making a living are perhaps more prone to deflection than people my age who have pared down demands somewhat. Films which tell a straight-ahead tale please us. They have a level of effortlessness about them. They are often quieter. Older films frequently understand, and revel in, the essence of calm linear narrative. *"In good films, there is always a directness that entirely frees us from the itch to interpret."* ~ **Susan Sontag, writer**

Typically, I show a set of four films. I try to thematically unite them in some way or at least emphasize how they might overlap in style. Intermittently I throw in a ringer, a film without an obvious link to the others.

Some months are set aside for specific genres. My recent attempt to show musicals bombed. Poor attendance as well as a technological glitch in the showing of the very appropriately named '**Calamity Jane**' has convinced me that I will henceforth only throw in a musical confection sparingly.

In November, because of an anticipated and incredibly predictable weather disruption, I plan to show only three films. In 2010, I presented, **The African Queen**, **The House on 92nd Stree**t and *(very nearly)* **Mrs. Miniver**. Each showed civilians coping with war *(The House on 92nd Street, a little less so but the propaganda value of its portrayal of the FBI was somewhat amusing and hardly understated.)* The African Queen was a very personal film that depicted its key protagonist, Charlie Allnut, a cranky Canadian expatriate with Denman characteristics, being dragged into a world conflict he had little interest in.

This November, Lassie, Bogart *(again)* and Hitchcock will fight the celluloid war on Denman. *"Pictures are for entertainment; messages should be delivered by Western Union."* ~ **Samuel Goldwyn**

The Denman Arts Centre is a lovely little venue to show classic films. Though my largest audience was a tad over thirty people, *(for a Doris Day film, a fact I'm still aflutter about,)* I have shown films at least once to just one viewer. If I get seven or eight people, it feels like a sell-out. Wednesday night, in addition to being 'Poker Night' and 'Meditation Night' as well as a night of any number of other activities, has also become classic film night.

If I brood at all about the limited turnout for my classic films, and I rarely brood about anything, it is that I am unable to infect people with my adoration of many old films. However, I am more than content to present a wide and hopefully intriguing selection. *"That was my one big Hollywood hit, but, in a way, it hurt my picture career. After that, I was typecast as a lion, and there just weren't many parts for lions."* ~ **Bert Lahr**

As much as our small Island is a cultural Mecca, it is also, occasionally, a minimalist public event practitioner. Film seems to have small currency: Old films have nothing much to offer us. I appreciate that. In my faster paced work life, popular culture was a touchstone, a shared experience that could bring people together. Old films, on the other hand, harken back to a time with which our ever-increasing population has little to connect. Literature similarly suffers from the onslaught of the new and shiny: kindles rather than books, downloads rather than small cinematic engagements.

I want to note, a historical nod at least, that back in the day, 1975 or there about, films were shown in the Community Club. Accessed from Pacific Cinematique *(as well as NFB shorts)* attendance was respectable and consistent. Subsequently, the programming was dispersed to private homes, homes not really able to sustain numbers.

Nevertheless, for as long as I am allowed to show old films, I will continue this placid pastime and trust the audience is entertained.

On Turning Sixty-Five

(an essay on my gently corrosive, intriguingly inevitable slide into an oblivion which I trust will be an age-friendly, buffoon-tolerant cocoon)

"It is a sobering thought, that when Mozart was my age he had been dead for two years" ~ **Tom Lehrer**

As 2012 uncorked, I was feeling a little pooped. Partly the flu, one of those undermining snivels that linger, that keep you half-way down, yet always glancing pensively up, optimistically eyeballing a better day. During this meandering malaise, I barely fulfilled my modest community responsibilities. At the core of my mounting melancholy, the brutal approach of the Ides of March, my 65th birthday.

Some months earlier, it dawned on me that I would be turning sixty-five on the evening of the March Open Stage. With that synchronistic bombshell, I volunteered to be the Guest Host. What a wonderful opportunity to totally humiliate my aging process, on the very night that I forever transitioned into the wood chipper of time. I would write witty little couplets for the evening, wry poetic ringlets, fastidiously funny fingerlings of poesy, exuberant essays on decline. I would sing the classics, all those depressingly trenchant songs about aging, not *'When I'm 64',* it's much too frisky, and I should have sung it a couple of years ago for I will never be sixty-four again. So, not that landmark ditty, but songs that reference the deeply textured passing of the years, that held some meaning for me as I withered on time's thin vine. *"Old age isn't so bad when you consider the alternatives."* ~ **Maurice Chevalier**

For some spell, I had sensed a personal musical drift back to the mournful sentimentality of that American icon, that actor and singer, that Real McCoy, Walter Brennan. I found myself enigmatically drawn to songs like '*Old Rivers*' and '*Old Shep*'. They are easily accessible on *YouTube*, in between licensing ineptitudes, that is. For a time, I spent hours singing along with Walter, or a guy who sounded a lot like Walt at any rate, bemoaning the loss of that fine dog, Old Shep, that weary farmer, Old Rivers. It was curiously painful to sing about Old Shep because I had never had a dog, had in fact planned to get one once I retired but, alas, still hadn't taken the pooch plunge. I like dogs well enough, but they require time and management. They need to go for a couple of 'walks' a day. I resist walking. I mean, just for the sake of walking. If I have a destination, walking is okay but I am as likely to join a walking club as I am to join a book club. I read randomly, inelegantly, somewhat like the way I walk these days. Restrained chaos!

Another song from the 50's also began to swirl about. Gogi Grant first sang it in 1956 but shortly thereafter, Tex Ritter performed a fine rendition of *The Wayward Wind*. Given March's vigorous weather occurrences, choosing *The Wayward Wind* to sing seemed downright prophetic. *"Old age is like everything else. To make a success of it, you've got to start young."* ~ **Fred Astaire**

Most reflective people reckon that it is not how old you are but how much life you have in you that counts. Apart from a few speculative risk-taking episodes, I have not lived an adventurous life nor been an earnest explorer. My days have been quiet and moderated. Nevertheless, even before I got to be '*getting on*', one of my more civic inclinations was to express myself, share my ideas. Choosing not to run about the village shouting out randomly seditious thoughts, I opted a number of years ago, whenever the mood struck, to write letters to the editor. That was escapade enough for me, uttering opinion, probing the world, groping for answers. Three years back, one of my letters to the Globe and Mail talked about baby-boomery.

"Dear Editor,
As a sixty-two-year-old and counting Canadian male, I have been meaning, for quite some time, to apologize for getting older. I have no one to blame but myself and, of course, my parent's bad timing back in the late 40's. They failed to understand that having me and my sister would burden future systems to

such a degree that governments would be hard pressed to manage the fiscal collapse they allowed to happen by pathetically inept regulation of greed.

I also blame my employer for tempting me with early retirement when I was a mere pup of fifty-five. They thought they could hire younger, quicker, faster and, ultimately, cheaper staff and allow me to wander off to whatever pasture I had picked out for myself. I can't thank them enough for their lack of foresight.

Even though I eat well and exercise, I imagine, with sufficient codling, I have at least twenty years left. Many on my little island are well into their dotage. We have a population cap that keeps out too many of the young. It brings me comfort, knowing I will be surrounded by peers as I grind, inexorably, to a halt."

This particular letter drew me into a fairly fleeting e-mail chitchat with the Globe's letter editor. My initial version was twice the size and she kindly asked if I could scale it down. As I age, I am increasingly adjusting to the theory, if not the practice, of scaling down so the exercise set a good example for me. The letter also struck a chord with at least one other publication that year, the Newfoundland and Labrador Pensioner, the organ of the retired civil servants of those most easterly Canadian outposts, which reprinted it *(the editor apparently liked my "in your face" tone)* to amuse their furrowed affiliates, no doubt all desperate for a late life chortle. ***"Aging seems to be the only available way to live a long life."*** ~ **Daniel Francois Esprit Auber**

In the end, I did execute the two songs (Old Rivers, and The Wayward Wind) at Open Stage with the able assistance of two Island musicians with a lot of pluck and the requisite sense of humour. Tension got the better of me during my rendition of Old Rivers and I forgot the lyrics. In the safe harbour that is Open Stage, I retrieved my notes and began again. It worked well enough. The Wayward Wind followed and it went off like a breeze. Still, I was a pulsating package of perspiration.

I am now firmly planted in my sixty-five-year-old boots and sandals. Though I will continue to warble from time to time, I also aim to crank out a few more darkly twisted observations on the humorous angst of aging *(assuming there is any,)* just in case there are a few of you who relished getting older unscathed.

A Treatise on How We Advertise Events on Denman Isle

"I should be sincerely sorry to see my neighbor's children devoured by wolves."
~ **Waldo Lydecker**

"Neatness, madam, has nothing to do with the truth. The truth is quite messy, like a windblown room." ~ **William J Harris**

On a soggy and squally February day, with thoughts of Waldo Lydecker on my mind, I went about a semi-regular activity for some of us on Denman, those of us with a poster or a scrap of information which needs a public pedestal, scurrying about on the Denman Island Bulletin Board circuit. Downtown Denman has a bounty of bulletin boards. Potted about the Village, usually affixed to what passes for our public buildings *(though some private enterprises such as the General Store and Abraxas generously provide space for notices,)* the bulletin boards of Denman are a constant source of interminable intelligence. On one hand, there are almost too many places to go to when you want to post your crucial crumb of data. On the other hand, this righteous communications objective, the near-viral promotion of an upcoming political event, or more frequently it seems these days, the leafleting of every available space with an announcement about an entertainment occurrence, would achieve, you might imagine, the ultimate educative windfall: every living human on Denman would know exactly what you were announcing and how much fun it would be. There would be no room for doubt, no room for someone to say, *'I didn't know that was happening. How come you didn't advertise?'* If only!!! *"The single biggest problem with communication is the illusion that it has taken place."* ~ **George Bernard Shaw**

Recently, a half dozen compatriots and I spent the better part of two months conceiving, designing and marketing an Audio Arts Collective project, Harmonica Spring 2012. This was a titanic step for our troupe. We were able to generate a lot of On-Island and Off-Island promotion, including the pièce de résistance, the front page story in the March Flagstone. We had signs, we had leaflets, we had buzz. The 'mini-festival' was also pumped up on at least three Island cyber-sites: The Denman Works electronic calendar, the Arts Denman website and *DenmanIslandInfo*.

Still, after all that, the concert, an engaging family friendly evening with an outstanding blues–playing bill of fare and first-rate goodies to masticate, had a restrained, almost disheartening attendance.

I mention this, not to curry commiseration, but to broach, for your consideration, the varied means by which we learn about events on Denman, the scope of those miscellaneous events and our facility to sustain them. Some events will fly, others will flap their wings ferociously yet fail to achieve a tolerable height. A few are for entrepreneurial profit, most are the consequence of non-profit labour. Within this organizational mélange, some preserve local capital in the community, others dispatch the funds off-shore. All create a measure of home-grown economic hullabaloo. *"I hear YouTube, Twitter and Facebook are merging to form a super Social Media site – YouTwitFace."* **~ Conan O'Brien, The Tonight Show (June 2009)**

Social media is an emerging avant-garde mass means of communication. What a marvel it is! Though I have somewhat mastered the premise if not the practice of e-mail, I was disinclined to set my sights on Facebook. Some years ago, I gingerly enlisted but quickly back-stepped, petrified that my long sought after forest of privacy *(fop)* might be compromised by an ill-considered word, a revealing notation. Having a tendency to run at the mouth, I was understandably fretful that I might blurt out some hitherto well-kept secret.

Once I was teleported to the Denman Island Bulletin Board, *(for those of you at sea over social media, the DIBB is an unpretentious internet rivulet whereby members can chat, post pictures and links (some pork, but mostly meatless, sausage) and is a sort of wired, over-the-back- fence information clothesline, or, if you are really a retro-romantic, a tousled party line,)* and realized I would have to jumpstart my dead battery Facebook life to enroll, I darned the consequences and hurtled in. As I write this, one hundred and thirty have registered. I now feel in the loop. Or noose! Or, at least, I feel like I am going around in circles in a slightly more informed manner. For example, I know that at least two dogs were recently lost, and, in a Nano second, found. Praise the Board! Additionally, all manner of political pursuits have been promoted. I plug my weekly Classic movies. Our Harmonica Spring workshops and Concert were frequently hyped in a caring and lovingly repetitive manner. *"Advertising is the art of convincing people to spend money they don't have for something they don't need."* ~ **Will Rogers**

March 2012 was a frenzied month for those with a need either to divert or be diverted. There were at least three classic music recitals, a number of musical gigs at our two key eateries, plus an assortment of other not-to-be-missed *(though I did, I'm afraid, miss quite a few)* amusements sprinkled hither and yon, including a couple of choice cinematic experiences. April is shaping up to equal or exceed the pleasure dome of distractions undertaken in March. We are an Island of one thousand, or so I've been told. I have rarely seen more than one hundred and fifty or so of us at any one time. While some of our playfully artistic activities are subsidized, most aren't. The citizens of Denman are indispensable *(indispensable, that is, in the sense that much of any prospective audience, by definition, are the, hopefully, deep-pocketed, glee-gluttonous, increasingly antiquarian folks of Denman)* to buttress these converging and occasionally competing leisure pastimes. *"Many a small thing has been made large by the right kind of advertising."* ~ **Mark Twain**

As you can tell, although this homily began as a reflection on how we advertise our entertainment and political wares, it has floundered into a broodingly parallel pond of impenetrability. Alas, I've scarcely skimmed the promotional surface, and miserably bungled completing my preliminary thrust, the etiquette and the efficacy of posting notices. Reluctantly, I sense another related article approaching. Consider this fair warning!

An Utterly Unamusing Meditation
(on Richard Cory, Bon Vivant and Suicide)

"I couldn't commit suicide if my life depended on it." ~ George Carlin

Most of my gentry codger-tations, though grounded in serious soil, weave languorously in and out of the loam of the preposterous and the paradoxical, or some cunning combination thereof. At the tail-end of March, a semi-soaked Saturday, whilst some Islanders were off the rock protesting the perils of pipelines and oil tankers and still others were hovering in Beethoven heaven at the Community Hall, I joined a wee cadre at the Arts Centre for a seminar to consider the subject of suicide. The intent was simple: explore how we think about the taking of one's own life, how we talk or don't talk about it.

I wasn't surprised that the turnout was low. Like most meagre mortals, I have my 'limited perspective' about certain subjects: for instance, the progression of what will surely be our humdinger of a Green Cemetery. While I have no doubt it may eventually be of some environmentally friendly benefit for my earthly remains, I have yet to build up a head of steam in planning for my expiry date. Others do, thankfully, and I may be eternally indebted for their grave efforts depending, I suppose, on the existence of the afterlife, another subject I avoid like the plague *(which, oddly enough, is a subject – epidemics of all types – that I adore blethering on about)*. I imagine most of us have our pet turf themes, or quicksand taboo topics we shy away from or embrace whole hog.

Suicide, for me, is another kettle of fish entirely. I am of at least two minds on the matter. Life, I believe, should always be affirmed, clung to with a gelatinous grip. The young in particular should be assisted to witness the contentment to be found in staying the course as one overcomes unpleasant, occasionally painful, temporary turbulences. Nevertheless, I also believe that when we adult humans have deduced that our time is at hand, and there is no other viable choice, we should have, under certain conditions, an unassailable right to exit, stage left.

But whatever I might think about the politics of suicide, the goal of this afternoon engagement was to permit the free expression of talking about suicide, primarily as a preventative tool. *"If I had no sense of humor, I would long ago have committed suicide."* ~ **Mahatma Gandhi**

As I sat there that Saturday, listening attentively, opining at the appropriate time, I divulged that my earliest smack-in-the-face recollection about the certainty of suicide was in my teens when the older brother of a relatively new friend killed himself in his old Chevy by running a hose from the exhaust into the sufficiently sealed inner shell of the car. I had seen him around; the friend was new; his suicidal brother was a couple of years older; they had a sister I was fleetingly setting my pubescent sights on. In short though, I never really knew him. After his death, my new friend inherited his late brother's wheels. On the night of our Graduation gala, six of us, three adolescent couples, drove up and down Vancouver Island, taxing the night, testing ourselves and, I suppose, experiencing the ephemeral numbness of unearthing juvenile thrills in what was, by some standards, a death car.

Later, however, I recalled that suicide had also made an impression on me some time earlier. It had dangled its uncomfortable inclination before me in grade nine or grade ten in the form of a poem, Edward Arlington Robinson's Richard Cory. *"Suicide is man's way of telling God, 'You can't fire me - I quit!"* ~ **Bill Maher.** Richard Cory, the poem, if not the man, is reasonably accessible. Cory is a prosperous fellow, an affable chap. By all superficial appearances, he has life by the tail. The four stanza poem ends with this stark summation:

> *"So on we worked, and waited for the light,*
> *And went without the meat, and cursed the bread;*
> *And Richard Cory, one calm summer night,*
> *Went home and put a bullet through his head."*

The impact, for me, on first reading, and on all subsequent readings, was, and remains, profound. The world can be a dark place. Affluence, admiration, all the trinkets one might covet, none will necessarily save you from your demons. To contemporize the point, Simon and Garfunkel, in the mid-sixties, were inspired to write a song about the life of Richard Cory. Van Morrison did a version of that same song. Both the poem, published in 1897, and the 60's folk lyric, accentuate the point made by the poet: life is a mystery; our own certainly and certainly others. Be careful whom you envy! *"You realize that suicide's a criminal offense -- In less enlightened times they'd have hung you for it."* ~ **Peter Cook, Bedazzled**

I was advised by my principal editor not to compose a piece on suicide. *"You write nonsense, for God's sake. There's nothing funny about suicide!"* I could muster no argument against the supremacy of her observation. Still, my primary way of exploring ideas is to document them, to poke at them diligently. The seminar ended with the expectation that those attending would become Suicide Talkers, people who would not shun the subject. In that vein, I proceeded with this small homage. As I did, I gave additional thought to *Richard Cory,* the poem. Was it still part of a prescribed curriculum? A contact in the Ministry of Education clarified that, within the English Arts these days at least, there are no mandatory poems. There may be sweeps, or at least, pockets, of Richard Coryites out there but the poem is not required. Pity! *"When you're young and healthy you can plan on Monday to commit suicide, and by Wednesday you're laughing again."* ~ **Marilyn Monroe, My Story**

By happenstance a film I was planning to show recently had a significant suicidal incident within the narrative. Though *The Heart is a Lonely Hunter* is fundamentally a poignant coming of age tale, a tale complimented by one man's tender journey through the lives of others, it was not spared the subsidiary sorrow of suicide. For there is, alas, always the real world. A smash of teen suicides by train in the suburbs of Chicago; a rash trio of apparently impulsive departures in Brampton, Ontario over the past year; a crush of suicidal exits of first nations citizens in the Cowichan Valley; a battery of youth suicides in the Comox Valley; the possible "political statement" suicide, Richard Cory-like, by a seventy-seven year old retired Pharmacist in a town square in Athens, Greece recently, and always, for me, though the memory of it does skip out of sight every once in a while, *Marilyn.*

Like almost all suicides, this article must end with no answers and nothing much to recommend it.

You're Pulling My LEG-acy, Right?

"Life is better than death, I believe, if only because it is less boring and because it has fresh peaches in it." ~ Anonymous peach farmer (possibly)

Shortly after my 65th birthday, the legacy requests started coming. Two arrived almost in tandem, like annoying, albeit euphoric, missionaries from lesser, but compatible denominations. Both were unexpected, and both had the objective of reformatting my relationship with their respective hosts. Both, I imagine, also seemed to hold me in some eventually much-more-beneficial-light than I was currently held. I was *their* future; *they* were my inevitable past.

I continue to expect more of these overtures although none have arrived thus far. These two may be it. I am not all that connected to the outer world. My fraternal organizational lifeline is relatively flat.

As for the two salivating emissaries, the first came from my one and only University, the second from my principal Political Party. For some reason, they both imagined that I might want to leave them something in their kitty once I had wound up my business on this corporeal coil. *"No legacy is so rich as honesty."* ~ Will Shakespeare

When I think of *my* University, I have very specific moments which call out. I was eighteen when I first trudged up to Simon Fraser University. The last thing on my mind was my mortality. Then, my life was before me, uncharted, remarkably blank, complex in its possibilities and thoroughly uncoordinated. Attending University was a rite of passage I barely understood. I had not been much of a student, either as a child or when a youth. I stumbled through my grades much like a drunk weaves his way home. Not for a moment in my formative years did I imagine I might attend an institution of higher, or

136

even moderately elevated, learning. Nevertheless, in September 1965, I became a Charter Student of Gordon Shrum's clever concrete Acropolis. As striking as it was, it leaked. My initial impression was of water seeping down numerous walls, indoors and out. The place was a sieve. Of course, my memory is also a sieve so there may have been fewer leaks than I imagine. Nevertheless, I expected more from a new edifice.

The times, fortunately, afforded me a swatch of other, more noteworthy memories, many of them political, a few quietly personal.

Regarding the fissures, plumbers and engineers, by now, have no doubt fixed them. If they haven't and I do leave the University something, I may designate the money be used to plug the dike. That would appeal to my sense of order, I think. *"We can't rely on people passing away."* ~ **Moe Sihota**

We *expect* universities to put the bite on their graduates. Alumni groups exist principally to keep the old school spirit percolating. School spirit costs moolah. Alumni Associations pummel their membership with invitations to fork over funds to perpetuate themselves, the elite, the proverbial cream of the crop. Opportunities are provided for the like-minded to huddle, swap business cards, network their way along the rocky yellow brick road. It is all very... *collegial.*

On the other hand, I have yet to hear from my various elementary schools. There were four, three public, and one private, the unheralded Bunny Hutch where I first dipped my toes in the puddle of formal learning. Later, there was my junior high alma mater, Woodlands, and the principled and principaled NDSS, my greatest academic torment. I don't know why public schools don't seek cash from generations of their graduates in the same way Universities fund-raise? Perhaps they do, and, thus far, have failed to track me down.

My political party of choice is another matter, however. I suppose I have led them on by being an ongoing member for over forty years. Even during its lowest ebb, and there have been a bunch, I have hung in there. A couple of years ago, NDP party president Moe Sihota candidly confessed that the BC socialist conspiracy was surviving almost solely on legacies from dead members and equally expired supporters. When I realized that, I immediately felt a little guilty that a.) I was still alive and obviously less committed than party ghosts were, and b.) I had not updated my will. *"Where there's a will, there are five hundred relatives."* ~ **Anonymous**

I have been amused by where the pitches *do* come from. Recently I was planning to watch a wonderful Australian mystery show on the Knowledge Network. I confess I am not currently a contributing patron. Perhaps I should be. There are so many things I *should* do. Nevertheless, just prior to the show commencing, the two erudite, well known hosts made their legacy gambit. They were speaking to any and all of us in Television Land to consider leaving a bequest so that future citizens who chance upon their particular version of public television programming will be sated. It was enticing. I almost picked up the phone. I *want* public television to continue. I also *want* to believe that there is television in the afterlife. I do not expect it will have new programming, however. The afterlife, if it has the tube at all, will, more than likely, have nonstop reruns of my least favourite show, My Mother, the Car. *"I don't even know how to spell 'legacy!'"* ~ **Ronnie Dunn, country singer**

This *may* sound selfish but I would like to end my earthly expedition as close to broke as possible. Timing is everything, right? I am, regrettably, frugal. I will scrutinize my pennies closely and fail miserably in a quest for a pauper's demise. With that in mind, and should I pass on whilst still a resident of this fair isle, I might well be tempted to share some of my post-mortal coil assets with any one of numerous deserving groups on the Island. At least *one* has sent out a general hint of how I (the greater I) might contemplate distributing the wealth. I sit, or have sat, on Boards who have benefited from the generous largesse of Islanders. Increasingly, rural communities will be discarded by government. We have no numerical value. That's why BC Ferries will never become part of the highway system and why fares will continue to spiral upwards. There are no meaningful votes to be had here. Proportionally, we cost *too much*. So, it will be up to the dearly departed (*US*) to fund our Islands future. Even in death, good citizenship is expected. *"Leaving behind books is even more beautiful — there are far too many children."* ~ **Marguerite Yourcenar**

Of course, all of this talk about "legacy" is damn depressing. It presupposes, oh, I don't know, one's expiry date. There are so many things you can't do when you dead, I'm told. One of the few benefits of death is that the last thing you will be worried about, assuming you *can* still worry, is your legacy. That's a comfort.

To the Victuals Go the Spoils… OR Food, Vainglorious Food

"My mother's menu consisted of two choices: Take it or leave it." ~Buddy Hackett

Food! When I was a kid, I never thought for a moment that food was a political hot potato. Okay, I didn't think much was political back then. But I do recollect periodical squabbles over food. I couldn't leave the table until I had finished what was on my plate. The rift then was fairly basic. My mother believed in 'waste not, want not'; I believed I should only eat whatever I wanted to. We frittered away little in our no-nonsense family, except for the amount of gratuitous time I squandered in staring contests with cold casseroles and semi-edible turnips. Invariably, I would cave and gobble whatever gruesome glop of food I had earlier spurned. My mother knew it. I knew it.

Contrasting these stern stand-offs was my mother's occasionally whimsical parenting style. As much as she was a product of an impoverished childhood where no fragment of food was ignored, she also hazily remembered her unfulfilled childhood food fantasies and occasionally allowed my sister and me to snack on our curious choices. Every so often, she would grant me my breakfast whimsy meal, canned chili con carne. Though my sister leaned toward tin-can ravioli, I was also not averse to succumbing to Chef Boyardee's succulent smelling pasta pops when it was offered.

As I grew older, my favorite snack became a hunk of raw onion accompanied by a sizeable slab of plastic Velveeta Cheese. Every year until she died, my mother would give me a Christmas block of Velveeta and one half dozen thin nylon socks. This rapacious ritual continues as I splurge every Christmas for a two lb. package of the yellow composite. I still have a few of

139

those thin, slippery socks so there is no need to replenish them. *"Red meat is not bad for you. Now blue-green meat, that's bad for you!"* ~ **Tommy Smothers**

My childhood memories of meat are few and far between. My favorite meal concocted by my mother was a noodlely, potato-festooned, sausage casserole with a pet name, long forgotten, she gave it, possibly slumgullion, slang for stew, but also apparently the name given to whale blubber offal AND a mucky residue from sluice mining. My mother liked the term and used it for a number of her culinary creations. Years after I left home I pestered her to remember the recipe for that fondly recalled casserole but it was gone like an eclipse of the sun. I can still evoke the smell and the sight of my mother's crisp, slightly scorched bacon, the pork fat swirling about the frying pan, slices of her homemade white bread being plopped in the pan to soak up the salty, sinful grease. I loved that oily coagulation. On the flip side, we also often ate the most gristle-laced roast beef this side of the Chicago stock yards. I was never in a position to challenge my parents about where they bought their inedible beef. The few steaks we ever ate were also fatty and fibrous, not like the deliciously juicy fat found in the crackling bacon but unpalatable hunks of tough cow flab unworthy of chewing. *"Ask not what you can do for your country. Ask what's for lunch."* ~ **Orson Welles**

My first significant gastronomic growth-spurt occurred when I moved into a pioneering urban commune in 1967. I was twenty and ripe for new dietary experiences. Co-habiting with twenty to thirty people, each with their own food preferences, was daunting. Though we were all for one and one for all, we had quite a way to go to develop a system of collaborative shopping and eating. It may have been simpler if we had all subscribed to one spiritual or political orientation. As it was, our two driving forces seemed to be a willingness to play a part in a hormonally driven collective living experience AND keeping our costs down. Our clustered communal co-existence demanded that we all compromise our tastes and develop menus which serviced the greater good, our unpretentious communal pocketbook. Alas and alack, we were exceptionally autonomous entities. Coincidental to our group adventure, the world was experiencing a taste-bud revolution. Initially, the only meal I was capable of cobbling together was a rather bleak, barely palatable meatloaf. This was my regular contribution twice a month, rain or shine for a couple of years. Eventually I moved, timidly, into the realm of vegetarian fare. It was a sluggish awakening. My key creation, then, was something called Nutty Noodle

Casserole. Though I had lost the recipe until very recently, it remains, sad to say, one of my singular life achievements. *"Vegetarianism is harmless enough, though it is apt to fill a man with wind and self-righteousness."* ~ **Sir Robert Hutchinson**

Years passed. By the time I left the Commune, I was, for all intents and purposes, ripe for a vegetarian life. I had pretty much eliminated meat from my diet by the early 1980's and, by the time I read Old Macdonald's Factory Farm in 1989, my course was set. The book elaborated in great detail how animals are raised for food on factory farms. I mention the book, not to proselytize, but to simply acknowledge what drove me away from the land of flesh-eaters. Now, aside from an occasional case of the shakes caused by fried chicken withdrawal, I belong to the loose-knit army of those who self-identify as 'vegetarian.' It is a motley crew and has many variations. I am a pitiable ambassador from a rag-tag faction who carelessly devour seafood, cheese, cow juice and the like. *"A man of sixty has spent twenty years in bed and over three years in eating."* ~ **Arnold Bennett**

I tend to fixate on a consortium of less than reasonable worries. For example, I currently have a lot of control over how my life is led. Certainly my diet is completely within my domain, except for those foods I am vociferously encouraged not to consume. Velveeta Cheese, as mentioned more than once, is on that list of contraband. Once a year I stubbornly continue to add it to my Christmas festivities.

But there may come a day when I have no control over what I eat. Vegetarians and Vegans, my kitchen kinfolk, may need to develop our own seniors housing in order to stay true to our food philosophies. In the dark of night, I fret over a catastrophic state of affairs, a time apparently closer than I wish to comprehend, when I may be so enfeebled that I will have to be spoon-fed, and have no say about what slop is situated on the spoon.

On the bright side, I am not dogmatic in the least. Ultimately, whatever the kitchen wind blows in will suit me just fine. If I don't like it, I will just sit at the table and stare it down. Like the child I once was, I will do whatever I have to do to get wheeled away from the table. Ha! Who am I kidding? I like eating too much. I ain't leaving the table until I'm done.

Vandal Love! <u>OR</u> "Well King, This Case Is *(Far From)* Closed."

"If you're going to hit a car, try to be sure that it's not a cop car." ~ **Judy Gold**

On the morning of June 14th 2012, I received a phone call advising me that someone had vandalized an RCMP vehicle which had been parked at the Denman West Ferry Terminal for almost a week. I had seen the car a couple of days earlier and been mildly curious about why it was there. I zipped down to the terminal and snapped a couple of pictures. Concurrently, on the Denman Island Bulletin Board, a 'conversation' had begun at about 7:30 that morning posing the cryptic question, *"Which is worse... RCMP on the Island or vandals?"*

I didn't particularly think the question all that watertight. Perhaps it was meant to be ironic. I doubt whether we have a choice to not have either cops or vandals. We have had other recent incidents of vandalism on Denman. Who generally perpetrates our vandalism or what possible motive existed for damaging the police car remains obscure. As for the police, though we have no resident officers on the island, there are times when the more judicious of us, contrary to the views of those who eschew any external oversight, might consider them fundamental.

Over the next few days, I mulled over the Bulletin Board discourse, added my progressively more orthodox thoughts, became unsettled at some of the categorical denunciations of the police and the sporadic gestures of support for vandalism, and, generally, pondered my own and others analysis of policing. My views are sufficiently nuanced that I then began to consider how they might have evolved. *"I'm not against the police; I'm just afraid of them."* ~ **Alfred Hitchcock**

At age thirteen, I met my first cop, not counting Sergeant Preston. I was playing *(dare I say it)* Cowboys and Indians with some friends in an empty field near my home. I was brandishing a decommissioned twenty-two rifle. The barrel was plugged. The cop asked me how old I was and what did I think I was doing. I meekly told him, *"I'm thirteen. And I'm playing Cowboys and Indians."* He fired back that I was too old to play with guns and to go home and grow up. My childhood came crashing to a halt. Okay, I embroider. I did manage to remain slightly childish for a few additional years and, occasionally, still revert back. Nevertheless, the rebuke stung.

Years later, in 1968, clothed in a calf length, surplus military great coat, longish hair flopping in a winter morning New Westminster breeze, I was pulled over by a squad car as I strolled along a sidewalk. The coat still had its shoulder insignias. It also had brass buttons down the front. After determining that I was not a member of the Canadian Armed Forces, they put me in the back seat and drove me to an isolated spot on the city's waterfront. They then compelled me to remove both the insignias and the buttons. *"You don't have the right to wear them,"* they declared. *"You aren't military material."* I already knew this awful truth, having briefly served in the Army. Once my coat was denuded courtesy of their handy police pocket knife, they drove off. I walked the two miles home to my commune. It took me a few days to work up the pluck to take another undisciplined march outside. ***"Only in a police state is the job of a policeman easy."*** ~ **Orson Welles**

By 1972, I was working in a teen drop-in centre. New Westminster had a husband and wife youth policing team in those days, Ed and Merle Cadenhead. They brought a resilient ethic of no nonsense support, care and concern to their job. I mention them because they were the first of many police officers I worked with over the next thirty years, initially as a youth worker and then as a social worker. Even though my few earlier experiences with police had been somewhat unsettling, albeit unremarkable, I generally found that the cops I dealt with were ferociously committed to protecting abused kids and ensuring that abusers were properly held to account. We often conducted joint interviews with children who may have been abused. The police usually led those interviews. They were trained to have a patient, methodical and solicitous style. Their matter of fact, plain spoken techniques served to help garner facts and build a solid case.

At the same time, I maintained a healthy skepticism about the formation of laws, how they change, or don't, and the nature of their enforcement. I was able, am able, usually, to distinguish between the makers of laws and those empowered and expected to fairly enforce them. *"Do you like being a cop?" "I love it, when it doesn't suck, sir."* ~ **Edward Conlon, Blue Blood**

So, here I am today, living on this small gendarme-less atoll. Though we have a small amount of crime, some likely unreported for an array of reasons, we have neither police station nor local cop with whom we can become familiar. Even though a number of families on the Island have police officers within their extended family, the RCMP is popularly viewed by a certain segment of the community as an alien entity not to be trusted.

A police car has been sullied, after sitting unmolested in plain sight for four or five days. As I write this, the matter is being debated in a number of quarters, perhaps the most visible being the electronic Denman Island Community Bulletin Board. Over twenty opiners have contributed, as of this writing, to the one hundred and one and counting postings. Within that modest yet dervish-like discussion is imbedded a medley of views about the police. A number are disparaging, some are balanced, a few even tolerant. Others are somewhat vague and non-committal. The conversation seems to have morphed from discussing one act of vandalism to expounding on the nature and character both of policing and its membership. Some of it is downright raw. Unquestionably, some residents of Denman harbour great pain stemming, it appears, from earlier, or current, interaction with the police. *"Can't we all... just... get along?"* ~ **Rodney King**

It may be indecorous to quote the recently deceased Rodney King. Nevertheless, he gained unsolicited notoriety twenty years ago as the archetypal target of police excess. Yes, I know, there are more grievous, and fatal, examples. However, his definitive message was a call for tolerance. While some on Denman seem to be able to muster forbearance and insight, we probably could do with a measure more. If there is such disparity amongst us regarding policing, the odds are we have pronounced differences on other issues, issues where we need meaningful debate and tangible results, such as domestic violence and affordable housing. Not surprisingly, there is some discord about what forum we should even use to debate issues of this sort, issues at once contentious, pressing and, from time to time, esoteric. I favour

DIRA as the forum; some are doubtful that DIRA does, should, or even could, reflect their interests; some have suggested a council of elders, assisted by preschoolers, which sounds not unlike the DIRA executive to me, who probably wouldn't say no to a savvy preschooler or two who had permission to stay up late to serve on the executive. Still others fancy talking through their hat, a time-tested way to win an argument.

"I Don't Read *The Flagstone*, SO THERE!"

"The newspapers! Sir, they are the most villainous, licentious, abominable, infernal - Not that I ever read them! No, I make it a rule never to look into a newspaper." ~ **Richard Brinsley Sheridan (1751 - 1816)**

Once a month for most of the last eight years, I have joined a small, relatively homogeneous group of Islanders' to collate the Flagstone, Denman Island's monthly periodical. We work in two groups: assembling, chatting, socializing. We typically finish the task in about fifty minutes. Afterwards, to observe the completion of our communal undertaking, as if we needed an excuse, we convene to a sitting room, nibble on goodies, sip a beverage and mull over a spider's web of current events.

Recently, conversation touched on an attitude, perhaps not prevailing but certainly simmering, which others and I have heard some folks express that they read neither the monthly Flagstone nor the weekly Grapevine. It seems to be, or so it is conveyed, almost a matter of pride with some folks, as if there is some inherent value, besides blissful ignorance, in not reading something so localized, so small town as our monthly gazette and our weekly spreadsheet.

We batted this revelation around for a time that particular evening before moving on to a more distressing, albeit distant event, the mall collapse in Elliot Lake, the resulting controversy over the cessation of rescue services, the uprising of local citizens and others appalled at that decision and the eventual reversal to a more aggressive rescue and, sadly, recovery attempt.

Later, back at home, I resolved to probe, or create in my gregariously gentrifying way, lore surrounding the reading and digesting of local news.

"Half of the American people never read a newspaper. Half never voted for President. One hopes it is the same half." ~ **Gore Vidal (1925 -2012)**

To begin with, I concede that the Flagstone is not, by most standards, a newspaper. Nor is the Grapevine! What they are though, at the very least, are reliable means, by rural standards, to regularly communicate information, ideas, news, both of a relevant, and, sometimes, a tad less interesting sort, on a more or less predictable basis. Both can be accessed by most anyone on the Island, by which I mean not only can we all read them if we so choose to but, with not a great deal of effort, *(witness my bumptious meditations)* each and every one of us can write for them.

This is a huge bonus. As one who compulsively writes letters to the editors of various national and regional papers, I appreciate not only those occasions when my opinions reach a larger stage but also the more compressed opportunity to survey local events; not just record them but plunge into them in a mildly humorous, rather more personal way. I savour the personal point of view and strive to weave bits and pieces of my life into most every article I construct. But the Flagstone has many other contributors, each bringing their unique flair, their particular perspective on our community and the world, to the collective mirror that the Flagstone most assuredly is. Additionally, the temperature of segments of the community can sometimes be gauged not only by letters to the editors, that collage of chirpy content, but also by the occasionally prickly uprising of distress over insert content and editorial decision-making. *"If you don't read the newspaper, you are uninformed; if you do read the newspaper, you are misinformed."* ~ **Mark Twain**

I am one of those, and I doubt I'm alone, who routinely reads the Flagstone from cover to cover. Though it is not, as previously noted, a 'newspaper' in the conventional sense, it is a record of our communal lives, capturing the constituent parts, the nitty-gritty, and the very occasional itty-bitty bikini wit, of our collective days down through the seasons. Though not a bird watcher, I can chart the comings and goings of flocks of flying fowl and those who focus upon them; though barely able to grow hair, I can read about the intricacies of local husbandry. And although the Internet is a constant source of exciting recipes I might consider trying, I read the Flagstone's cooking column to peruse local gastronomic trends. *"I read about eight newspapers in a day. When I'm in a town with only one newspaper, I read it eight times."* ~ **Will Rogers**

At the age of eleven, I became a paper boy for the Nanaimo Daily Free Press. Golly jeepers, did I love that job. For the four years that I delivered papers on 'Route 66,' I was a hustling bustling bundle of entrepreneurial energy. Six days a week, after school and on Saturday, I would join a half dozen other paper delivery kids at a small, slightly warped wooden garage located a block from my house. The newspaper leased it from the homeowner as a paper drop off/ pick up point. It also served as a bit of a hangout.

As a *paper kid*, I felt professionally obligated to read the news I was transporting. This early hankering to know what was going on around me has lasted a lifetime. This early career path came to an exciting end in 1962. I sold enough subscriptions to win a junket, along with a brigade of other paper kid capitalists, to the Seattle World's Fair. By then, I had turned fifteen, other areas of attraction were emerging, and I moved on. *"The newspaper is in all its literalness the bible of democracy, the book out of which a people determines its conduct."* ~ **Walter Lippmann**

There is a compelling correlation between the production and distribution of local news and a spirited citizenry. The writers, publishers and assemblers of the Flagstone are, not surprisingly, intimately involved in the honeycombed hum of our community hive. Earlier periodicals, the *"Rag and Bone"* for example, were also produced by people very immersed in their community. Some remain engaged to this day.

If there are those who deliberately avoid staying informed about our small community, it is not for the want of trying by others. And, truth be told, those who eschew local news organs may have other sources of information: conversations, voices in their head, Facebook, Twitter, bumper stickers, placards. There are more information wellsprings available today than at any other time in the memory of man, which is all to the good given our aging population combined with a growing demographic, world-wide, who shortly, no matter how many Harry Potter books are hawked, may be pathetically unfamiliar with newspapers and books.

To be a healthy community, a number of fundamentals are required, not the least being a free press. Even in our rustic and rambunctious hamlet, that requirement is an essential. Hence, I will continue to read and treasure the Flagstone and the Grapevine and the authentic, if occasionally fractious, beacon they both shine on our Island.

Helmet For Fury - One Prong of a Much-Forked Tongue

Part 1 – performed at the Readers Writers Festival July 2012

"Don't get it right, just get it written." ~ James Thurber

Every year it's pretty much the same for me, an intense tea-potty-like turbulence about what to do! What to write! What to read! A basket of brittle artistic angst erupts in me, a quixotic quest for something evocatively edgy yet still comfortably inconsequential to prattle on about at the Readers and Writers culture crawl! This year, I questioned if perhaps the Festival deserved a stay of execution from my lethal verbal musketry. No, I was told, enough already with your egalitarian urges, you're a writer. Fire away. Primed and loaded, the question then became, how to distill a volley of unprocessed, moderately deviant, semi-droll, potentially poignant pablum into an engaging twelve minute spoken salvo? One habitual hurdle: most of what I write is usually either too long or too short. Life journeys can also seem either too long or too short. Noses similarly are often either too long or too short. There is no perfect nose length, no perfect length of time to be alive. Any perfection there is, whether in noses or in longevity, or, for the sake of this exercise, in an essay, is the eventual actual length, no matter how long or how short each turns out to be. We take what we can get, right? Life! Noses! Essays!

Not necessarily so! People do reconstitute their snouts surgically. Some of you may have had just such a procedure; there are quite evidently some handsome beaks here today. As for life, there is, I suppose, a cosmetic surgery equivalent, cryogenics, the beguiling behaviour of freezing a body in some dried ice cylinder until, or if ever, there is a cure for whatever mortally afflicted the departed.

As for essays, especially those overstuffed with an excess of flower and flourish, well they often hop up onto an editor's examining table, to be wisely whittled away until they are but robust, albeit excised remnants of their former flabby selves.

But, back to my perplexing process of producing something worthy of being read. Most writing should have context. A smidgen at least! I am extremely fond of context though rarely have any to spare.

Last year I offered a slight story about a plague of pre-adolescents, youthful semi-savages living in small town pandemonium, bit player refugees from the William Golding opus. I was reaching way beyond my grasp. Mine was no 'Lord of the Flies.' More like 'Bored of the Flies.' Later, some wondered if I was feeling murderous given that the young scallywags in my story, emphasis on STORY, tried to throttle a near-do-well acquaintance. No, I reassured them, I was not in a homicidal frame of mind. I remain not homicidal to this day, at least no more than usual.

But developing something alluring, something provocatively original to recite at the Readers Writers Festival can test one. *"The base of my skull was showing. I have absolutely no doubt about it. I'd be dead without that helmet."* ~ **Bob Rogers**

Finally, close to the end of April, a fine half-sunny day, I thought I had found my topic du jour, something to hang my hat on. Helmets! That's right! You heard me! Helmets! Like, in case you hadn't noticed, the one I am wearing. *(a cheap gimmick, I admit!)*

I often ride my old bike. I always wear a helmet. I have bought into the frequently fractious notion that wearing a bike helmet is a reasonably clever thing to do. For safety, right! Touch wood; touch plastic.

Did you know there was a recent Supreme Court challenge against mandatory helmet wearing? As I understand it, the litigant believed that everyone should be compelled to wear a helmet, not just two-wheeler travelers. That fine point aside, one only has to spend a summer's day watching the bicyclists of Denman flaunt their ferociously pro and anti-helmet proclivities to know that the wearing of helmets on Denman is discordant. Some bicyclists wear them. Others don't. The message is explicit. Helmets are optional. You are free to risk serious head injury. No one will interfere. It probably won't ever be questioned except, perhaps, at the Readers/Writers festival, or at a coroner's inquest. *"Jerry Ford is a nice guy, but he played too much football with his helmet off"* ~ **Lyndon B. Johnson**

Personally, I was an easy sell about helmets. I spent most of my teen years growing up in an old house with a six-foot basement. For much of that time, I was *over* six feet tall. I always had to try to remember to duck. Being an incurable head banger, I often failed that vital memory test. No matter how wary I was, I was forever banging my noggin on the beams that supported the rest of the house. We didn't wear bike helmets then. Who knows how much damage was done to my progressively dented skull. Was it parental neglect? If someday I do explode into a murderous rage, I may well have to blame my parents, that too short basement and, possibly, an indifferent government without the foresight to decree that all unnaturally lanky kids wear helmets in squat cellars.

However, I find little reassurance in the notion that the government could have compelled me to wear a home helmet. My father abandoned his treasured '*Socreds*' because they made wearing seat belts mandatory. God knows what his reaction would have been to forcing people to stick their heads in plastic buckets, in their own home yet.

As with many things, I am of two minds on what level of intrusion I will tolerate from Government. I will however, continue to wear a helmet for each of those two minds, just as a precaution. *"Do as the Olympians do. Wear a helmet, even if you're not an elite skier or snowboarder - especially if you're not."* ~ **Dr. Roald Bahr**

As I began this writing mission, it was a sunny day, a day worthy of some outside activity. I had some wood to chop and stack. Chopping wood the way I do has inherent risk. I habitually wear sandals and shorts. Flying fragments of freshly split firewood can crush toes, batter shins, cause blood and scabs and pain. I sometimes use an ax with a loose ax head. If not handled properly, an ax head can become a noggin-beaner. I began the chop-fest wearing my bike helmet. This added measure of skull protection seemed logical especially given my unsuitable summer attire.

151

The day warmed up. I kept swinging; scooping; stacking; swinging; scooping; stacking. My head was a sweat box; the helmet, a torture chamber. The ax handle remained secure. Ants, spiders and wood bits were flung in the air like grains of rice at a wedding; a few pummeled the helmet; decisions had to be made!

Finally, I conceded that the helmet was just too damn hot and removed it. I continued swinging. It was a mulish exploit considering the risks.

As I whacked away, I imagined what the optics might be if I were to sport the helmet at a meeting. Any old meeting! Meetings grow as prolifically as turnips do on Denman. It's not a new thought. It might have an impact, make a statement. Most Denman meetings are relatively safe. Oh, ideas are lobbed into the air from time to time but they usually don't have sufficient weight to be injurious. Still, sometimes they smack you in the head with surprising authority.

Would wearing a bike helmet everywhere raise awareness of bike and wood-chopping safety concerns? Perhaps, coupled with a snappy slow island slogan like *'Let's not get a head of ourselves... wear a helmet!'* Or not!

Porta-Potty Punditry - The Second Prong of a Much Forked Tongue!

Part 2 - presented at the Readers Writers Festival July 2012

"I write to discover what I think." ~ **Joan Didion**

I suppose I knew quite early in that I would have to get away from the helmet motif and, to keep my creative head above water, make a thematic leap into a deeper peripheral pool. Prior to the conception of this oeuvre I stumbled across two prominent Islanders scouting out territory in the back of our miniscule business district. *"What ho, Citizens?"* I hailed. They continued on, deeply ensconced in examining serious community affairs. Eventually they explained that they were looking for just the right place to locate a discretely situated Porta-Potty.

Immediately I felt blessed. Here was a companion subject to complement any notions I might develop about helmets. *"Her secret was as safe as a fly in an outhouse."* ~ **Anne Sexton**

Not so long before, I had been twiddling my projectionist thumbs in one of our more artistically inclined quasi-community buildings when I was buttonholed by a slightly tortured soul seeking use of the facilities water closet. Of course, I relented Johnny-on-the-spot. Anyone who has spent more than a few minutes on Denman knows that we have an appalling biffy shortage.

Don't get me wrong. Well, do if you must, but I'm not letting the cat out of the bag, or the Community Hall, where a caterwaul of them reside, or did until the recent renovation project, when I say that you almost have to KNOW someone before you can use a washroom in Downtown Denman. Or be a registered attendee at one of our premiere events. On that note, here's another feline in the knapsack escapee note; we have a serious water and septic problem here on cloud nine. More than that, we have what I have been told is a failing infrastructure. We have no viable political system that I am aware of able and willing to deal with larger septic and water issues. Our local governments, the intractable Trust and the coagulated Regional District to be precise, each appear to have limited interest in addressing Denman Village's fomenting sewage concerns. Both are flush with our tax dollars, awash with our liquid greenbacks, and likely have no yen to tap that well. A recent meeting of the Trust seemed more preoccupied with ensuring that their exceptionally long minutes were as perfect as they could be even though the thankless village water works riddle was referenced. They spent over fifteen minutes that particular morning fine-tuning the official record, three minutes longer then each of us here has been given. *(n.b. local writers get twelve minutes to read their work. If I am the yardstick, this may be thirteen minutes too long.)*

"I found out why cats drink out of the toilet. My mother told me it's because the water is cold in there. And I'm like, how did my mother know that?" ~ **Wendy Liebman**

Most people who live here have their own means of addressing pressing biological function. We do make some feeble accommodation for unaligned visitors. There are indoor privies potted about which a whining self-absorbed tourist can make use of if they stumble on the right party, some soft-hearted native willing to extend themselves. We also go to a not inconsequential bit of extra trouble to provide Porta-Potties in the summer. Our motto might well be **Yes We Can**. Obama has taken that maxim about as far as he probably will so it may be up for grabs.

So, on that late April day, I inserted my annoyingly-haphazard thought process into the conversation the two distinguished citizens were having about where to locate a new summer Porta-Potty. With a dedication and focus I could only aspire to, they deftly ignored me. Left to my own modest devices, I was able to glean that the logistics, not to say the aesthetics, of *'Loo Location'* are convoluted. The Village of Denman is small and compact; by one measure, nothing more than a paltry whistle-stop on the speedway to the Mecca of Hornby. If one is going to place a P-Pot where it is accessible, one might also want to consider privacy. This is why many of us have toilets in our homes.

Privy privacy is a given in most abodes depending, of course, on the size of the family. On the other hand, if you plant the commodious contraption deep in the trees, or so far out of sight that you have to convene a safari to find it, well, you've hoisted yourself on your own privy petard, haven't you? *"There's always a little bit of heaven in a disaster area."* ~ **Hugh Romney aka Wavy Gravy**

As I considered the emergence of portable sanitation pods on our planet, their very nature, their core, I easily recalled when I first became aware of them. I was in Toronto in August of '69. Woodstock was on the horizon, only a few hundred miles away. My unadventurous spirit, however, was complacent, too content with the sprawling stimulation offered by the vast city of T.O. I dragged my feet until September and, by then, the essential weekend of my generation had passed into the coffee table history books.

In 1970, to mollify my appalling lethargy, I went to see Woodstock the Movie, probably the finest documentary of its type ever. One of the main non-musical luminaries in the film was the porta-potty guy. There is a captivating two-minute snippet in the movie that is devoted to his special skill set. I can find no accounting of how many of the devices the organizers had but if you consider that there were 500,000 people at Max Yasgur's Farm, well, you do the math. What you may not know is that this two-minute interview of Tom Taggart, the porta-potty guy, led, some years later, to a lawsuit based on *"the grounds of mental anguish, embarrassment, public ridicule, and invasion of privacy."* Though the law suit eventually failed, Tom Taggart's somewhat involuntary but congenial contribution captured not only the schism that permeated the 1960's but offered a tonic for tolerance and eventual healing. In April, 1970, a New York Times writer, Craig McGregor, reviewing Woodstock, the Movie, described Tom's, and perhaps America's, predisposition to endure when he said, *"And the man who is the real schizophrenic hero of Woodstock, the Port-O-San man, who empties the latrines of the beautiful people ... has one son there at Woodstock and another flying a DMZ helicopter in Vietnam."* *"My name is only an anagram for toilets."* ~ **T.S Eliot**

I could go on, time permitting, which it never does. You may wonder, surely there are more worthwhile subjects then helmets and porta-potties to ponder? Of course there are! As a writer, I also delight in opining on the larger issues of the day. War! Peace! Oil! Coal! Physician assisted –suicide! Paintings of a nude Stephen Harper! Even though Woodstock is long gone, its spirit of chaos and community sputters every now and then. In two days, this urbane urchin offshoot, this divine diversion will be dispatched to the record books. It has been my privilege to highlight some of the smaller disregarded scraps and slices of Denman life which resonate for me, subject matter frequently less traveled, much like an overgrown forest path next to two roads diverging in a yellow journalist's wood, themes like the Bramble that is the Helmet dialogues, the Gordian Knot that is Denman Village's spectral septic symposium! That's where I have chosen to tramp today. Thanks for keeping me company.

A Willful Winter Walkabout!

"I am of the opinion that my life belongs to the community, and as long as I live it is my privilege to do for it whatever I can." ~ **George Bernard Shaw**

In a land once removed, a friend, an unassuming sentinel with a rather dry, dreamy deportment *(that is the way I took him,)* talked about sweeping an uncomfortable issue which I had been, and now he was to be, quietly engaged in, *"under the rug."* I took it he was suggesting what he might well do *(or was considering he might well do,)* would primarily be motivated by a chivalrous spirit to shield his community. Finding himself unexpectedly inheriting the prickly horns of this troubling dilemma, his protective first instinct was that his community did not need to go to the harrowing woe of tackling yet another unpleasant, likely irreparable, fact of life. For the sake of this sonata, the particulars are immaterial, though I appreciate how obtuse this might seem. What is of importance is to note that those who find themselves concerned with unpleasant or provocative 'ethical' issues demonstrate a level of cautious circumspection, a diligence comparable to the qualities we trust they display in their personal lives. *"Call me a 'rube' and a 'hick', but I'd rather be the man who bought the Brooklyn Bridge than the man who sold it."* ~ **Will Rogers**

In any community, vexatious distractions are part of the day to day gravitas of human experience. Most days, we go about our business in a rather matter-of-fact way. Many of us, I suspect, not especially wanting to endure extremes, seek a measured pace, a restrained regularity. But random exigent events do sometimes get the better of us: acquaintances come face to face with domestic upheaval, economic circumstances implode, health becomes compromised, ideas become entangled. Caca occurs!

157

Some of the discourse centering on the evolution of the community occurs in the shadows. On any given issue, only a few are usually involved in rigorous planning. Even processes which are transparently public are typically shaped by a sturdy few. Though a common theme in our excitable community is the clarion call for transparency, often no amount of lucidity is ever quite enough. The cable ferry chronicles seem to me to not only have been cluttered by way of too many clumps of corporate kitty litter but also infused with a palpably clichéd narrative. As expected, many islanders seized the least enthusiastic stance possible. Though the process allowed for a spool of circuitous discussion, and as full a vetting as a post-Sarah Palin, Vice-Presidential candidate should have to endure, it was always rather clear that the Board of B.C. Ferries would be the ultimate arbiter; the resolution would be their business decision to make. The final report came back to the community, in late November 2012. While it engendered some routine ersatz commentary, for example, a member in good standing *(I would hope)* of the Denman Island Father Time Club *(my membership application is, sadly, still in the hopper)* held aloft a sound-bite size placard with the scythe-sharp mono-morsel, LIES, which was, interestingly I thought, not just a tenaciously thrifty analysis, but also the title of one of the late Stan Rogers more beautiful ballads. The evening served its primary purpose, to allow a little coal-fired steam to be released and thus terminate the extended proceedings with an enriching exhibition of hamlet mystification. *"Never miss a good chance to shut up."* ~ **Will Rogers**

This question slips into my lexicon quite frequently; do struggles ever end on Denman? Is there ever any acceptance that a protest has run its course? Am I even allowed to ask these questions? Of course, I'm allowed to, I suppose, but will tongues titter *(or twitter)* because I have expressed some unease about orthodoxy on Denman? Is there any sense of noblesse oblige *(admittedly an elitist grace)* within our pedantic parish? Do I expose myself to criticism or worse *(which might be either excommunication or the more lethal ambivalence)* by stepping off the conventional sidewalk? *"People's minds are changed through observation and not through argument."* ~ **Will Rogers**

Of the glut of issues which have, of late, injected their needling toxin into the public tableau and garnered some modest traction, one which has the avant-garde potential to stretch tolerance to bungee cord length, has been the mostly counter intuitively named technology, *Smart Meters.* For some, the idea of a state utility wielding a micro-waved missile and metaphorically plonking it into our noggin without real consent is a tad pushy. For others, perhaps a few the likes of your ragged correspondent who assume so much damage has been already done that the point of no return was reached years earlier, the subject is a snoozer. As with many topics in our small, relatively blinkered, backwater outpost however, the *Barely Smarter than a Fifth Grader Meter* issue is fraught with explosive-laden potholes. Wise travelers, certainly wiser than I, will take a more discrete path.

On the other hand, an acquaintance recently described her experience with the Smart Meter installation process. As hers was being installed a swarm of neighbours gathered to express their displeasure with her and the installers. She implied that the whole experience had a surreal quality to it not unlike the scene in the classic movie Frankenstein where the inflamed villagers, operating with little information, much fear and a Skookum script, chased the inelegant *(albeit imposing)* monster through the village and into the countryside. *"When they are alone they want to be with others, and when they are with others they want to be alone. After all, human beings are like that."* ~ **Gertrude Stein**

There are times when I ponder the peril in expressing an opinion, especially in print. Though opinions are certainly useful and expected, they oft times, especially if they go against the communal grain, tend to kindle extreme reproach. If Denman had an Opinion Cap, similar in some respects to its retrograde Population Cap, is it possible that we might be the better for it?

This column was composed chiefly during the tail-end of a recent bout of the flu. I am, by my own reckoning, much more candid when in the grip of aggravating bodily malfunction. Fever-driven sincerity is not necessarily accuracy. Though health impeded my attendance at the November 29th Cable Ferry translucence, news coverage occurred almost before the actual event and allowed me to buoy up my insight. And, as it turns out, the Cable Ferry imbroglio is probably still giddily percolating. That seems to be the way of most really durable issues. They possess the resilience of healthy young zombies, they never truly get resolved, and they are eternally available to bolster the independent spirit that muscles our Islands 'Body Politic'.

Up and Down the Garbage Chute

"I've been married to one Marxist and one Fascist, and neither one would take the garbage out." ~ **Lee Grant**

One of the last things I ever anticipated having much time for (some have observed that there are many things my mind doesn't readily snap to attention to) were thoughts of *garbage*. Garbage has simply never risen *high* enough on my aroma radar. Though I was not immune to its persuasive bouquet, it has usually held short sway. Even when, on occasion, I was compelled to haul heaps of domestic debris by borrowed pick-up to the Coquitlam Transfer Station *(if one didn't know better, one would think transfer stations are places where you change buses)* I pinched my nose and tried not to look too closely at the wanton waste being 'transferred.'

Then I retired and moved to Denman Island. Here, as on most Islands, waste is given more consideration than I would have thought possible, or preferred. For instance, we have no neighbourhood 'transfer station.' I am told there once was such a place. Or maybe it was just an embarrassing old dump, a potential future historical site. I have also been informed that some islanders used to throw junk off the old dock into the sea, perhaps prematurely planning to thwart future cable ferry designers. *"My trash can got stolen five times. Finally, the owner just let me have it."* ~ **Jarod Kintz, A Zebra is the Piano of the Animal Kingdom**

The current routine of Denman refuse removal is not so different from the city, where, as I recall, it was a fairly matter-of-fact, more effortless distraction. Here, on this sanctified soil, there are added levels of complication. For example, I'm older then I once was and I have to haul my can *(the one with*

160

garbage in it) up to Lacon. Intermittently, I drive it up the hill, committing, in one fell swoop, both an environmental and a physical fitness atrocity. More often though, I drag it like the ball and chain it is, an irksome weight to challenge my increasingly geriatrifying bones.

Another hitch I face, that we all face I suppose, even if we are not keen to admit it, is *what* to put in our garbage receptacles. In the city, recycling is *almost* an option. You *can*, or you can recycle. No one is really watching, other than CSIS, that we know of. On Denman, especially in the summer, the flood of islanders hurrying to the 'Depot' sometimes seems to me to be a particularly twisted rural rendition of 'The Stepford Wives'. When I go there, I feel like an ungainly, out-of-sorts Rosemary's Baby. On any given recycling day, I watch my neighbours allocate their glass, plastic, paper, and metal into what they hope is the right receptacle. Some do this with the deft aplomb of a cocksure lemming, others seem awkwardly blitzed by the diverse decisions they are called upon to make. A few waffle, perhaps concerned that a wrongly chosen bin will be their insidious undoing.

And then there is the additional cost. In the city, my taxes paid for garbage collection. Here, there is a user fee. In the city, I might leave a case of beer at Christmas for the Waste Management Technicians. Or, at least, think about doing that if I remembered. Here, I have resisted leaving alcohol of any denomination on the side of the road. *"If I have any appeal at all, it's to the fellow who takes out the garbage."* ~ **Lee Marvin**

I learned to recycle somewhat late in life as an urban communard in the early 1970's. Those meditative days under the tutelage of K.W., a husky, expatriate German carpenter, have lingered with me way beyond their past due date. He forcefully guided our cumbersome collective towards the inspired separation of materials years well before it became socially de rigueur.

Garbage disposal had, by then, petrifyingly imprinted itself on me. I was not easily able to make adjustments. It seemed that my parents, themselves shell-shocked by an increasingly complex world, had adequately prepared me for the future. Not!

As a child, I was not expected to interface with garbage. That was my father's purview. My meagre allowance was not pegged to the removal of the family refuse. In fact, it wasn't pegged to any expectations at all beyond the

161

washing and drying of dishes. As I cherished the caress of soapy, greasy water on my mitts, doing dishes was almost a spa-like joy. I compulsorily rotated these two tasks with my sister, more for her dishwashing discomfort than for any egalitarian sibling motive. She loathed washing dishes and squirmed with palpable pre-adolescent heebie-jeebies when it was her turn to stick her fingers into the oily slosh.

Aside from a clear memory of the family heritage garbage can, a small white canister, perhaps with a small foot pedal to raise the lid, sitting on a shelf next to the top of the stairs that led to the basement, I have no recall of my childhood garbage removal years. *"My wife is always trying to get rid of me. The other day she told me to put the garbage out. I said to her I already did. She told me to go and keep an eye on it."* ~ **Rodney Dangerfield**

With the foggy bifocals of hindsight, I now know that neither of my parents, (both bred on dirt poor farms, my mother's family especially relegated to an immensely impoverished landscape,) would have had any childhood familiarity with refuse. Gardeners both, they would have composted pretty much everything. Every scrap of anything remaining would have likely had a reusable value. *"Waste not; want not!!!"* How often I heard that consumer intolerant axiom, especially as chanted by my thrifty mother!

Of course, being a boomer baby, it took a while for the mantra to take hold. Children, at least those I knew, were feted with the benefits of the post-war boom. Plastic was the future. Everything was artificial. For it to have value, it *had* to be packaged. Competing messages pummeled my confused generation. *"One woman's trash is another man's treasure."* **Slightly reworked proverb**

The politics of waste disposal are, reportedly, heating up again. Change, always a bugbear for Denmanians, is afoot. Our waste may not be wanted. Our recyclables seem set to suffer from an infusion of BIG recycling policy, courtesy of MMBC (which sounds like a news network, doesn't it?)

Speaking of the city, rubbish dumping has taken on epidemic proportion. A recent newsflash explored how kind and thoughtful citizens are leaving all manner of totally useless items at various Sally Ann depots. One can only suppose that they believe they are being charitable. An even more recent report tells of rogue recyclers out in the Fraser Valley plundering similar, albeit apparently more redeemable, 'donations' like thieves in the dark of night, extracting anything they deem worthwhile.

Such desperate, urban altruism would *never* infect Denman. Here, surely, we believe that, just as it takes a village *(or a downtown)* to raise a child, it also takes an entire community to continue to talk turkey, or tofurkey if you are so inclined, about how we redistribute our trash.

My Last Picture Show!

"Oh how Shakespeare would have loved cinema!" ~ **Derek Jarman,** *Dancing Ledge*

In my somewhat fiscally challenged, casually misspent youth, I dwindled away an autumn and part of the following winter residing in a colossal city back east. I was aimless in those days, curious, awkward, ever seeking something of worth to do with my life. As the days darkened, my lack of structure began to press in. I started attending all-day cinema houses. Over the next few months, I watched an astonishing number of sundry films. This extreme, hour upon hour, days dribbling into wasted weeks marathon of movie-watching not only developed an appreciation in me for the diversity of vision to be found at the movies but also provided pretty clear bits of evidence that I needed to *'get a life'*. I dallied in that eastern metropolis till deep December and then repaired back west.

Though it took me quite a few additional years to get my life on track, I continued to be irresistibly drawn to film. *"Film as dream, film as music. No art passes our conscience in the way film does, and goes directly to our feelings, deep down into the dark rooms of our souls."* ~ **Ingrid Bergman**

Once I came to Denman Island, I was partially taken with the notion to show a series of dark, gritty urban films to my new community, this dark, pretty, rural sanctuary we share. Then as now, I was obsessed with the smoky glow of sinister cities.

164

Whilst an infrequent weekend resident, I had occasionally attended films shown in the Activity Centre Gym. This entrepreneurial exercise eventually concluded sometime after we moved here permanently *(nothing to do with us, I should point out)* and, for a time, there was a public celluloid vacuum. Subsequently, with the evolution of the Arts Centre, a Sunday Movie Night program was cultivated. This too wound down and the celluloid vacuum resumed. My little stage was set. It was, initially, a narrow stage. As mentioned, I rather boringly, egocentrically, wanted to show only film noir. That was my brilliant, volunteer business plan: to show black and white dramas set in distant cities. *"Academia is the death of cinema. It is the very opposite of passion. Film is not the art of scholars, but of illiterates."* ~ **Werner Herzog**

After pitching my plan to Arts Denman to present a series of classic films in the Arts Centre, and determining that Wednesday evening, though not the most advantageous of evenings, might be the more consistently available, I proceeded to line up an initial sequence of films. The first movie on my marquee, in late September, 2007, was **Naked City**, an excellent noir and a film that captured the sweltering New York City summer of 1947. I followed up with another tremendous noir filmed on location in the New Orleans of 1949. Both of these films embody one of the great things I enjoy about watching films made on location; films shot out in the streets harness a vibrancy, an immediateness, a rush of realism that can give, and retain forever, a riveting documentary-look. It may also have been that I was missing the buzz of city life and film noir can capture that threatening, intoxicating hum.

In the spring of 2008, I switched it up and began to present more traditional classics including two of my all-time favourites, **The Best Years of Our Lives** and **To Kill a Mockingbird**. Over the next few years, I offered almost one hundred and fifty magnificent and enduring classic films. *"One thing I know for sure. A person can't sneeze in this town without somebody offering them a handkerchief."* ~ **Genevieve in The Last Picture Show**

On a couple of very special occasions over a duo of successive summers, I was asked to show films that specifically suited a larger entertainment theme. For one, a Martini Lounge extravaganza, I was asked to show a few gangster/prohibition films as a provocative lead-up to the opening and closing night of 2011's Natasha's Gin Joint and Cabaret. The third film, **Love Me or Leave Me**, a wonderful and dramatic 20's era classic with Doris Day and

Jimmy Cagney shown three nights before the *Speakeasy* themed event garnered my highest ever turnout. Thirty plus people attended. This was a benchmark I was not to surpass. I still marvel at the hold Doris Day seems to have on the people of Denman.

The second occasion, a year earlier, was a chance to play a small part in the Social Service/Art experience, 'There's No Place Like Home,' a fundraiser for Home Assist, one of a number of essential programs of the HDCHCS, on which I now serve as a Board member. My small part was showing two charming Judy Garland films, **Summer Stock** and **The Wizard of Oz**.

"John Bernard Books: Damn.
Bond Rogers: John   Bernard, you swear too much.
John Bernard Books: The hell I do."
~ **John Wayne and Lauren Bacall in conversation in 'The Shootist'.**

Time has moved on. June will be my concluding month of classic film presentation. I will show four wonderful western tales. **Ride the High Country**, the first June western, is also an immaculate ode to the passing of time, to the gut-wrenching transformation of the west.

The second film of the month will be the elegiac and dusty **Yellow Sky** with Gregory Peck and Anne Baxter. This film has a wonderful connection to Denman. It features the first stunt riding performance in film for current island resident, Martha Crawford Cantarini. The third film will be a similarly dusty little film, the exquisite Henry Hathaway directed **Rawhide**, with Tyrone Power and Susan Hayward.

My final exhibition will be John Wayne's swan song, **The Shootist**, also starring Jimmy Stewart and Lauren Bacall. As with Ride the High Country, there is a definitive theme of finality, an inevitable passing of time about The Shootis' that I find powerful, compelling and, dare I say, ever timely.

As I write this small requiem to classic films, I realize that, in ending my brief run, I will need another Wednesday night diversion. Perhaps poker?

In any case, it has been an entertaining hoot. My heartfelt thanks to all who came out, or planned to come out to enjoy my now dissolving retro cinema, but got distracted.

The Secret Societies of Denman

"- You said this wasn't a cult.
- Secret society. There's a difference.
- Not from where I'm standing.
- Then take a seat." ~ **Jennifer Bosworth, Struck**

The genesis of many of my Gentrified Soul articles is often an idle thought - *I am fraught with more than my fair share* - which won't quite keep still any more. Some take forever to write, forever or even longer. Others compose smartly in a matter of hours. That is the way it was with this undertaking. Recently, an assembly of associates was cogitating on the woolly world of cults along with other matters I should add, *(so you won't think we were fixated)* and their historical infiltration into a tiny wedge of the food-services industry. Earlier that evening, I had playfully opined on the secrecy *(and if not secrecy, then the lack of public awareness)* of the Denman Ukrainian Dinner which I have attended most every January since I arrived on Denman. I don't recall ever reading anything in the Flagstone about this premium cultural event *(though it might have once been a footnote in that long defunct column, Misinformation,)* and implausibly posited that it was akin to a 'secret society'. When this pedestrian observation fittingly got short shrift, I mulled over what other groupings of people on my adopted Island also flew under the Flagstone, and, presumably, the public radar. *"Most secret societies...are collegiate. Or adult... They are like fraternities, only they don't have houses or public identities. In colleges, their members are usually local, not national, but the adult ones tend to be more serious and on a larger scale. We don't actually know what they do. Because they're secret."* ~ **E. Lockhart**

167

First though, I needed a working definition to give my provocative proposition some legs. I selected the following Wikipedia excerpt: *"Alan Axelrod, author of the International Encyclopedia of Secret Societies and Fraternal Orders, defines a secret society as an organization that is exclusive, claims to own special secrets and shows a strong inclination to favor its own."*

Armed with this handy, relatively benign, working definition, I began to eagerly hypothesize. What first occurred to me, putting aside the fine, furtive perogy feast I attend most years, was that the Island is rife *(how rife is open to speculation, perhaps by the National Rife Association)* with a loose confederacy of secret societies, all pretty much engaged in the same activity: READING. Hogwash, I hear you say, unless you are a water conservationist. But take a moment to reflect. Have you ever experienced a conversation with a self-confessed BOOK CLUB disciple who was panicking over their failure to research the latest mandatory obligation of membership? The torment and guilt are a heartbreaking exhibition to behold. The impression is that many of these Book Clubs *(you notice they generally are generic in name...aka THE Book Club... so you have no idea where they are located or who else might be a member)* are indefatigable in their fervour that members toe the line, to read that book, to tote that bale *(apparently a specific requirement of certain rural, agriculturally oriented book and hay-baling clubs.)*

In their defense, secret society Book Clubs may not be totally unwholesome entities. Many people function best if they feel they are distinctive, engaged in the noble and highly discriminating act of reading a taxing work, have innocuous yet comforting 'special secret' rituals such as determining which obscure novel or, god forbid, non-fiction opus, they will next coerce their supplicants to read and report back on *in detail:* all of the garish gratifications of a shared literary encounter. Additionally, Book Clubs seem to demand a mind-boggling allegiance and regular time commitment, all Protestant work ethic values much admired far and wide, particularly in the countryside, where many people smugly profess that they enjoy arising to the cock-a-doodle-do of a neighbour's rasping, albeit rhapsodic, rooster. *"Bursar?" "Yes, Arch Chancellor?" "You ain't a member of some secret society or somethin' are you?" "Me? No, Arch chancellor." "Then it'd be a damn good idea to take your underpants off your head."* ~ **Terry Pratchett, Lords and Ladies**

Sticking with secret Book Clubs, in the ten years that the Denman Island Readers/Writers Festival has been in existence, the agenda has never, to my knowledge, embraced a discussion of the pros and cons of Book Clubs: never even mentioned their existence. Yet I think it fair to say that a good percentage of those attending the Festival either actually belong to a Book Club or secretly yearn to. Why all the mystery, I wonder? How many secret Book Clubs are there on Denman? While there is no way of knowing exact numbers, *(the Canadian Census, most recently completed in 2011, fails to capture this data which, given the Conservative Government's fresh dispatching of the Gun Registry, is no big surprise,)* I believe there must be at least six Secret Society Book Clubs operating with impunity, selecting only those folks whom they wish to, engaging quietly, behind closed doors, in the relentless autopsy of numerous, unnamed written works, and, finally, profiting from the social spoils of belonging to a closed corps of bibliophiles. *"You're probably wondering what sort of "secret society" I'm in. Well, I can't tell you much, but I can tell you it's not the Skull and Bones, the Masons, or the Cacophony Society. No, this secret society is so secret that I'm not even sure I'm a member. I can tell you the group I might belong to calls itself "The Whispers," and takes its secrecy very seriously."* ~ **Jarod Kintz, I Should Have Renamed This**

Unlike Book Clubs, which are obliged to be selective, the annual Ukrainian Dinner actually admits non-Ukrainians, though how an unaligned body might find out about it is unclear as its existence *(prior to this expose)* has not been generally publicized. Nonetheless, one and all who attend are expected to declare their ancestral minutiae and relate some picturesque ethnic episode; those without the requisite Ukrainian *(or broader Slavic)* credentials customarily draw on their own usually modest cultural pursuits; most in attendance are, none the less, amused. Though attendees are, superficially, treated equally, all and sundry are aware, if only because of the mounds of holubsti, paska, perogy, kutia, and a sea of borscht, that being Ukrainian is the incontestable cat's meow. *"I've heard there's a lot of bag piping in that house. I'd love to go check it out." "So...you want to join the secret society of revolutionary plumbers."* ~ **Benson Bruno, Evergreens Are Prudish**

I have only skimmed the surface of the secret society trend on Denman. By their very nature, surreptitious social enclaves exist, and thrive, often, but not always, in the shadows *(and with all the trees on Denman, there are plenty of shadows.)* It may be that many of us belong to a clandestine collective and, if true, then we are all invested in maintaining this covert, not to say convivial, conduct.

Stand-up Comedy? Hmmm, I Wonder!

"I think it is the duty of the comedian to find out where the line is drawn and cross it deliberately." ~ **George Carlin**

Recently, I got an e-mail announcing the imminent explosion of STAND-UP COMEDY on Denman. My first thought was, *on DENMAN? SERIOUSLY? On DENMAN?* I mean, it didn't take me long, once I had settled here, to assume that the term **OCP** stood for ***Outbursts of Comedy Prohibited.*** Right! I mean there were by-laws for everything. It wasn't hard to believe humour had been outlawed. Not enforced, mind you, just banned. But then, once I acclimatized, I figured that, no, that's too harsh. What the Trust and the guffaw-a-minute Denmanian masses probably really mean by **OCP** is... ***Official Comedy Plan...***but nobody had quite got around yet to forming that committee; or, perchance, reviving some erstwhile, mothballed, shuck-and-jive, yuk it up, dissident, ersatz 'merry pranksterish' oyster festival sub-committee.

Consequently, I was tempted by C. Urquhart's e-mail. Even if it turned out that all she secretly wants to do is fashion a new, improved comedy committee, you know, a Comedy Advisory Planning Committee to counsel the Trust on arcane matters such as zoning schemes which fail to meet an acceptable environmental happiness quotient, that are simply not joyful enough. Life is so depressing in our rain forest. If government can't cheer us up, who else will? I'm a committee sort of guy. That would be right up my alley, you know, if we permitted alleys.

We *MAY* permit 'alleys.' I guess, in the country, they're called trails. I do know that, every once in a while, when I am having my obligatory urban flashback, on account of all that acid rain I absorbed in the city, I pine for back alleys. One of the great pleasures I had in the city was meandering down neighbourhood lanes, taking a peek into people's yards, not in a voyeuristic way, well maybe, but more in the vein of people watching, except it was my own quiet, back-yard analysis project. Well, you can see, by this little alley-oops distraction, that it is incredibly easy for me to lose my comedic way, even though comedy is in my blood. *"Comedy just pokes at problems, rarely confronts them squarely. Drama is like a plate of meat and potatoes, comedy is rather the dessert, a bit like meringue."* ~ **Woody Allen**

I come from a highly amusing family. My mother was always jolly. Like, when I was a kid and I'd be her default straight man, I'd say, *"Mom, I'm hungry!"* And she'd look at me, her blue eyes watering from fits of hysterical chuckling, and start laughing again. Daft-like. And then she'd say, *"Oooooooh, my little man's hungry! Get me the can opener, Willy,"* she called me Willy a lot, and that often gave me the willies, and then I'd get our can opener, one of those old ones that you had to jab into the can and pry your way along until you either cut yourself on a jagged edge or, miraculously, got the can open. She'd plop the contents into a Melmac bowl *(yes, to all of you Alf fans, a plastic bowl made on the planet Melmac)* and then chuckle away as I dug into the cold beans.

The thing I always remembered, especially when shovelling into my cold, but lovingly served, legumes, my Mom may have chortled a bit too much, but she always fed me. Thanks, Mom.

So, you can see why I was enticed by the stand-up comedy e-mail. *"I actually was class clown, but I don't know how that happened because I've never been considered an outwardly funny person - as the people in this room will attest."* ~ **Janeane Garofalo**

We all have impulses. Ever since I was kid, I have wanted to be disruptive. Not in an *'I-have-a-really-great-cause-and-demand-that-the-world-change'* way; more of a *'pay-attention-to-me-this-stuff-is-boring-wasn't-that-little-bon-mot-of-mine-funny'* way.

But can Denman cope with a constellation of 'class clowns?' Remember, we have a troupe of teachers who live here, many retired, a few not. No doubt all of them are painfully familiar with the ubiquitous 'class clown.' Their edified eyes must be rolling at the thought of stand-up comedy getting a toehold on the Island. Even though the management of class clowns in the school system has now evolved to a high art, an epidemic of buffoonery on Denman, even if contained in one evening's entertainment revue, must spawn a terrible sense of déjà vu for that demographic.

Will they try to undermine the initiative? Or, more perversely, dredge up any long repressed urges of their own to commit an irrepressible act of tomfoolery? *"While awaiting sentencing, I decided to give stand-up comedy a shot. The judge had suggested I get my act together, and I took him seriously."* ~ **Tim Allen**

So, what is comedy? And why are comedians essential to the social fabric? Comedy, at its optimum, helps us sidestep solving problems. In that sense, comedy is not unlike most committees. Committees are often set up to obscure a problem in a bog of process. Comedians like to crack jokes to take our mind off of problems. You can see the similarity, right?

Whether committee or comedy, the question becomes: what are Denman's humour needs? Or, perhaps, given the sheer size of that brainteaser, I should ask, what aren't? Are there verboten subjects a Denman comedian simply shouldn't touch with a ten-foot variance? I'm thinking, for instance, that coal mines are about as droll as a dead canary. And any hilarity about a potential theme park launching on the Island likely wouldn't make a big splash. And though I have always thought that the Denman economy would blossom if the Feds built a penitentiary here, well, I can see that the humour potential movement for that brain wave would be zilch.

Then there is the 'Islands Trust.' In the past, I have been known to take witless pot-shots at it. For many, however, the Trust *is* a sacred cow. Which reminds me, another sacrosanct subject might be people's dietary practices. Whether they consume the not-so-sacred, run-of-the-mill bovine, or eschew flesh of anything except the mighty artichoke and its ilk, most people take their diets uber-earnestly and are affronted by frivolous banter which besmirches their culinary orientation. As it should be! True taboo territory! *"I don't want to be 60 years old standing on stage telling some jokes. I want my life to mean something."* ~ **Steve Harvey, humanitarian AND host of TV's Family Feud**

I think I have sufficiently scratched any itchy hankering I had to *commit* stand-up. Writing intermittently semi-amusing pieces here and there, and occasionally discharging an awkward, mildly clever aside at a meeting, gratifies most of my clownish cravings. I hope we have a juggernaut of jokesters who stand up and are counted when the time comes. I'll be there, in the audience, appreciating whatever crop of comics can be harvested on Denman. Laughter is always nourishing.

A Can of Worms... Unleashed!!!

With apologies to those living or otherwise engaged whose words I have quoted with unauthorized accuracy in this quasi-artistic activity.

"I am not sure if I should open this can of worms, but here goes. Why do people move to an island and then want to change it???" **Perplexed Island resident opining on DIBB some months ago.**

Ah yes. Worms. Cans of the twitchy little critters! CASES! Not only do worms apparently come in tin containers, they can literally be manufactured on the head of a pin and shipped with almost no investment, no measurable infrastructure, to anywhere in the world. Cans of worms have a number of intriguing characteristics, a principal one being that they can suit most occasions. For example, the fearful anguish that some people move to Denman with nothing but horrid change on their mind. Like jolly buccaneers, these newcomer-brigands pounce off the boat, jiggle nickels and dimes around in their fancy-pants pockets *(likely not pennies as we have moved into a post-copper era in more ways than one)* and immediately herald, 'Things have to change here. We have to shake this place up.' And, before you can say, *Bob's-your-smelly-old-can't-leave-well-enough-alone-gentrifying–uncle,* they start to agitating like there is no tomorrow, like the tomorrow we have always come to expect, a tomorrow that looks pretty much like today, not to mention how similar it should be to the way yesterday appeared, is on the endangered species list.

Ah yes. Worms. *"Life is hard. Then you die. Then they throw dirt in your face. Then the worms eat you. Be grateful it happens in that order."* ~ **David Gerrold.**

174

Even before the posting on the Bulletin Board, I had been thinking about them a lot. Worms, that is. Not necessarily cans of them. And it wasn't just the squiggly 'mechanics' inherent in the proposed *new-fangled* Green Cemetery. Once I am a goner, I expect I will have little or no vested interest in how my girth is disposed of.

To stay on that tack though, if I am to be permanently polished off by a whopping wiggles worth of worms, I wholly anticipate that they will do it with a minimum of fuss. I also fully expect that they will be locally grown, reasonably sized little fellows, not some imported strain. The thought of being devoured in the prime of my death by, say, the bootlace worm, aka Lineus Longissimus, a humongous creature which has been known to grow as long one hundred and eighty feet, sends mortifying chills down my eventually decomposing spine. Death should be a journey, a bit of a cruise to the Outer Islands; not an imported, B-grade horror movie. *"It is infinitely better to transplant a heart than to bury it so it can be devoured by worms."*
~ Dr. Christiaan Barnard

But, back to worms as *metaphor,* and *change* as a can of them. Some may resist the pure genius in likening the raising of a discussion on change and how it presents itself *and* the sinuous, slightly inscrutable image of wiry little worms-of-thought squirming around in some enclosed container, a can, say, or a brain. When one mentions *opening* a can of worms, one is likely suggesting that there will be an entire worm farm of disparate opinion. The impression derived from using the expression 'a can of worms' is that worms are always oppositional, that to think that two worms will agree on anything, aside from their mutual desire not to be found on a fisherpersons hook, is beyond the pale. That impression, of course, is ludicrous. No one knows what a worm thinks. Especially another worm.

But the sad, boring truth of worm uniformity should not be permitted to subvert a popular and incredibly useful figure of speech. And, truth be told, given that there are, ostensibly, hundreds of thousands of species of worms, there may well be copious circumstances where worms of very separate stripes step on each other's toes, so to speak, where their slippery, mucous-dripping carcasses cross paths, or trails. Incidentally, trails are a whole other...can of worms. *"We are all worms, but I do believe that I am a glow worm."* ~ **Winston Churchill**

Though some believe the original expression, *can of worms*, was an articulation of disquiet from simple fishermen, lugging their garden-dug worms in a can down to the old fishin' hole, having to somehow control the critters as they clung tenaciously to their earthly clump of life, *this* particular can of squirminess references a trepidation, its true genesis somewhat imprecise, that the last half decade has produced a clarion call from urban-rattled 'newbies,'; a 'demand,' as it were, to have a police presence on Denman. Is this 'fuzzy' thinking or something more tangible, you might wonder? The reality is that we do have police on the Island. Though not permanently stationed here, they are here frequently enough to warrant radar and driver's licenses 'alerts' from helpful town-criers who feel compelled to advise those who have some difficulty obeying the fundamental tenets of citizenship and responsibility, to take the long way around so that their dearth of driver's licenses, insurance, seat belt usage, registration or sobriety will not be penalized. There was even the implication recently that the police were somewhat to blame for a Hornby cat named Bob hightailing it from a car during a police road check. *"Change is inevitable - except from a vending machine."* **~ Robert C. Gallagher**

Though the sentiment which spawned this querulous column was an ill-measured but *well-liked* Facebook remark that those who move somewhere new should simply *accept* 'what is' as the way it should always be, I have difficulty accommodating the implication that the community one finds upon arrival should solely be determined by those who came before. What an onerous obligation! Still, no doubt, this was the thinking of our many pioneer families, those old time pre-1970's Denman residents who were willy-nilly tossed around in the surf by the great unwashed hippie wave that rolled ashore in the late 60's. *"Why would you move here if you don't understand where you moved?"* **A very recent comment on DIBB by another perplexed Island resident.**

It *is* awkwardly amusing to hear over and over again the proposition that those who are new to a community should abstain from altering it in any way beyond, of course, the novelty of their basic existence. Historically, immigrants who have self-exiled have fought to retain some flavour of their first culture. The Canadian experience, much like the vaunted American immigrant experience, has been to melt us all into one big legal pot, all the while fostering a patina of multiculturalism and equity. Some, rightly, take issue with this.

But it is sluggish summer now. Most of our worms are busy at work in the garden, along with, no doubt, a few agitating snakes in the grass. There is, nevertheless, always a chance that an errant can of worms might spill over in the next while, seeking some wiggle room. Though I doubt this article will worm its way into your affection, I'd be thrilled if it did.

Two Solitudes... At the Very Least

*"Rural towns aren't always idyllic. It's easy to feel trapped and be aware of social hypocrisy." ~ **Bill Pullman***

Spring had shot by. Summer thoughts were beckoning. Every so often, I stepped outside and breathed in the satisfyingly sweet air drifting down from the Beaufort hills. I felt a wave of ennui sweep over me as I inched into the summer of my sixty-sixth year and anticipated its inevitable winter. I found myself spending a lot of time *worrying*. This is not an unusual condition for a moderately meditative man. We are obliged to worry about the ever-deteriorating state of the world, and if it is not really deteriorating, then, perhaps, it is merely adjusting. Shifting! An image comes to mind of a slightly world weary earth, hitching up its pants, setting itself in order to accommodate change.

And as I gave some reflective thought to the world, I paid a little bit of attention to myself, to my loved ones and the community in which I have found myself. Occasionally I have been asked, as many are, I expect, *'How did you come to be here?'* This question is usually posed in a social situation. I habitually respond with a rote answer. *'Serendipity,'* I say, quite often, though I do zest up my answer every now and then with some excessively laudatory exquisiteness such as, *'why, this is the best place on earth,'* or, with a token PET shrug of the shoulder, *'just lucky, I guess.'* And I believe each and every answer. Still, there was a hint of a search involved. We didn't just land on Denman without giving it *any* thought. That would have been utterly reckless. *"I was brought up in a very open, rural countryside in the middle of nowhere. There were no cell phones. If your lights went out, you were lit by candlelight for*

178

a good four days before they can get to you. And so, my imagination was crazy."
~ **Juno Temple**

Even without our raft of weekend expeditions to find a place to live out our years, we weren't especially fastidious. There was one aspect of small community living we didn't examine closely. It was that decompression of consciousness you undergo as you float up to the surface of Mayberry.

My reality, the compendium of experiences which had framed me and all my true-life source material, has stemmed from the undeniable fact that I have lived most of my adult life in a city. My reference points were urban. My skills, my fears, my approach to the world all flowed from the unending series of cosmopolitan pressure points that had punctuated me daily.

It wasn't always thus. I was raised in a small town. Nanaimo was almost the whole world when I was growing up. I knew its borders, I knew all the best swimming holes, I thought I knew its pulse. If you are relatively stationary for the first few years of your life, especially in what has to be considered a much simpler time, you come to believe that where you are is all that there is.
"Nostalgia is not what it used to be." ~ **Simone Signoret**

Recently, I stumbled across a Facebook site called *'You know you are from Nanaimo when...'* It has well over six thousand members and is full of marvelous history, photos, remembrances, observations, melancholy. While I have contributed a few small thoughts, others have posted a wealth of records, historical documents, anecdotes and such.

What I have mostly taken away from this particular internet museum is that I now know that I knew my childhood community hardly at all. My existence in the heartbeat of my hometown barely registered. This shouldn't have come as a surprise. On the more global stage, most of us are barely pebbles, or, to strain the metaphor, grains of sand. Still, this awareness of how lives were led by those with whom I grew up, or those who came before or after, leaves a sort of emptiness in me. While it is much too late, and agonizingly pointless, to wonder if my coming of age could have been different, I do have a new appreciation for the complexity of life. Without social media, I wonder if I would be asking these questions in quite the same way. ***"Twitter is a great place to tell the world what you're thinking before you've had a chance to think about it."*** ~ **Chris Pirillo**

I fret about my addled addiction to our local social media. Perhaps, you might opine, that it is not really an addiction? Still, similar to a number of others on our small Island, I spend a fair amount of time getting information from this impulsive source. I scan The Denman Island Bulletin Board for a sense of the ebb and flow of intelligible fluidity on Denman. It is an interesting means of communication. Some favour it more than face to face intercourse. Social intercourse, that is. And why wouldn't they? It is an immediate medium. And the ability to see your thoughts bounce around in cyberspace is intoxicating. You think, *'Did I actually say that?'*.

Opinion can be expressed at the press of a button. Once there in cyber-print, it can seem to become more substantial, more thoughtful, more *'Wow, I actually did say that?'* Borrowed ideas can be posted that give a sense of ownership, of wisdom. Images from elsewhere which capture a momentary flash of insight can be borrowed and disseminated. To refashion a homily, *'You are what you repeat.'* **"I think maybe the rural influence in my life helped me in a sense, of knowing how to get close to people and talk to them and get my work done."** ~ **Gordon Park**

Occasionally, I would wander into a large city park. The trees would hover above me like giant hoodlums waiting to mug me. Clearly, I had to escape. As much as this urban hallucination drove me into the country, I have also come to dread being mugged by virtual hooligans. It is especially concerning when they live in my real Island community. As brilliant and informative as social media can be, and I have little doubt it often is, there is an uncomfortable obscurity about it. Even if you know the commentator, there is an aspect of ambiguity, a vagueness. As close as we think we are connected *(with that curiously alienating cyber-connectivity)* we ultimately exist, each of us, in our own solitude. Real community demands safe engagement. Social media, especially local social media, has a ways to go to prove that it is one hundred percent safe, accurate and of any lasting value.

Commuting With Nature

"I wake up every morning at nine and grab for the morning paper. Then I look at the obituary page. If my name is not on it, I get up." ~ **Ben Franklin**

It has been said to me on a couple of occasions, mentioned in the way particular people occasionally stress a suggestion they have, not necessarily people such as my late father *(whose less endearing idiosyncrasies I might emulate someday, if not already)* who constantly told the same stories over and over, honing them until they were letter perfect, so much as people who are enthusiastically, insistently repetitive, who simply have to get their brainchild across. My friend knows I will write about *almost* anything. He thinks he has the ideal column for me. After decades of intimate, indoor toil, much of it working at home in his spacious study, the times have delivered him to a white-collar job which requires the most substantial of sacrifices, at least from my slothful perspective, to wit, *a morning commute*. He revels in it. He now has a community with whom he shares the dark of the morning, the companionship of the commute, the smell of the sea and that most tempting of voyages, a ten-minute sail *(or rather, motor, and, perhaps, a soon to be ingenious BC Ferries version of tug-of-war)* across the sound to Buckley Bay.

"They are great people," he says, *"the skillful, jaunty crew, the throng of morning travellers. We are almost like family."* I believe him! *"We have become very close,"* he adds, *"We, ferry crew and passengers who attend the 6:40 am ferry most every week day."* *"I know,"* I reply. *"You are like a family. That's great. Enjoy every moment of it,"* I underscore. And I mean it. I *really, really* mean it, I muse silently to myself in my best Sally Field voice. If you *have* to catch the 6:40 am ferry day in and day out, there had better be

181

something about it you enjoy. *"I feel sorry for people who don't drink. They wake up in the morning and that's the best they're going to feel all day."* ~ **Dean Martin**

I totally believe that he is passionate about his communal commuting cabal, almost as passionate as I am about staying in bed until I bloody well feel like getting up. On a recent Tuesday following a long weekend, visiting family got up at 4:30 am in order to catch the indispensable 6:40 am ferry. I could hear their footsteps plodding in the morning darkness, packing up their guinea pig menagerie, clomping every which way to find their traumatized cats who desperately didn't want to get out from under the bed where they spend way too much time as it is, and who certainly don't want to be crammed into their travelling cages.

While I couldn't get back to sleep, I resisted getting up to bid them adieu. I wanted to though, and *almost* arose to pay my respects, or help lug a compliant guinea pig *(and are there any other kind, I wonder?)* out to their car. But I was giving it some thought only for the most self-centered of reasons; if I did get up, I might very well try and beat them down to the ferry and inject myself into my friend's 6:40 a.m. morning commute still-half-asleep-social-club. I decided to be selfless and stay in bed. *"I wish I could commute to work by roller coaster."* ~ **Anonymous**

Unfortunately, I still had my little *reportage* problem. I *wanted* to write the commute column. In point of fact, I had already started it. As it was, I was uncertain where it was going. *Or where I was going.* Did I actually have to get up one morning before it was...seemly? It didn't seem so. Do war correspondents *actually* have to go to war to write about conflict? Were there 'war columnists' who simply opined about war without putting themselves in harm's way? Was getting up to catch a 6:40 a.m. morning ferry akin to putting oneself in harm's way? I was all over the map on the question. Full disclosure, I do keep a map under my pillow for just such geographically ethical questions.

This disgraceful debate with myself went on for months. On the few occasions when I had to go to Courtenay, the nearest commercial district to our isolated outpost, I seriously considered rising before the full effects of my required beauty sleep kicked in. Common sense prevailed and I maintained my somewhat lethargic, attractiveness enhancing routine. *"There is no hope for civilization which starts each day to the sound of an alarm clock."* **Anonymous**

Eventually, the day arrived where my personal needs and my literary needs unavoidably converged, conspiring to foist the 6:40 ferry upon me, or, rather, me upon it. The result would, of course, be the same. I held out some faint last-minute hope that I would simply sleep in because my electric alarm clock, part and parcel of my once high tech radio alarm clock system, had failed some months earlier and had yet to be replaced. Alas, I have reached an age where sleep is not as deep as it once was, where the body insists on being at the ready just in case the grim reaper chances by.

I awoke at the unfamiliar hour, stumbled through a semblance of my morning routine, hobbled to the car and drove through fog, internal as well as external, to the ferry slip. The string of lights along the community dock glimmered as if it was Christmas. I was almost alone. I twiddled my thumbs. Other friends arrived, two solo voyagers also thrusting themselves into the shock of painfully early departure. I waited in my car, looking for the commuters. Cars dropped off shapes. Shadows drifted by. Eventually, it was time to drive on to the sturdy Quinitsa, Denman's beloved but doomed ferry. I boarded. *"Looking for a new job at the moment, but I know the 6:40 and 7:20 are both popular commuter ferries."* ~ **Comment on DIBB**

Once the vessel sailed *(so to speak),* I strolled into one of the Spartan passenger lounges. There was no one. I went to another and there was my friend with a number of his fellow travellers. I sat opposite, made small talk, feeling somewhat alien from this tight-knit group of commuters. They could obviously sense that I was a fraud, a sightseer, a pretender.

I had hoped to embed myself in the 6:40 am morning commute cult, much like a war correspondent might. As it turned out, I was just a window-shopper, a morning dilettante, a voyeuristic dabbler. I briefly socialized as one must, kibitzed a tad, smiled my bearded, knowing smile and moved on as the ferry approached Buckley Bay.

A few short weeks later, the 6:40 a.m. ferry came under the careless aim of the culture-killing Liberal Government. My satirical shots were nothing compared to the economic bloodbath poised to be visited, apparently, on the 6:40 a.m. Denman morning commute.

Flu-Idle... OR Perhaps, Idyll!

"When we played softball, I'd steal second base, feel guilty and go back."
~ Woody Allen

I suppose I have spent much of my life feeling guilty. As a kid, I did things that always seemed to generate the pugnacious question, "Okay, who did that?" It was usually me, of course. Whatever the crime, I was the kid with his hand in the cookie jar. I was perennially handy, and, thinking back, I was learning a useful skill, how to be unabashedly guilty.

In Grade six, I scored on my own team during a lunch time, pick-up school-yard soccer game. It was one of my first ever opportunities to score in an intramural setting and I botched it big time. After that episode, rather than being proud of my moment in the other team's sun, my interest in group sports spiraled into oblivion. *"Calvin: There's no problem so awful, that you can't add some guilt to it and make it even worse."* ~ **Bill Waterson**

I have just spent this past week *(the week of January 8, 2014 and counting)* being shockingly sick with the flu or, as I often embroider it, a delirious mix of pneumonia, typhoid, cholera, and any other near-fatal afflictions you might care to name.

In this terribly congested time, I have also had to manage a series of waves of guilt over missed obligations. To add to my culpability, my erstwhile 'guilt complex,' I began the weekend, Sunday January 12th to be precise, by attending a new fun activity, a local writers group. Perhaps I should have stayed at home but I'd been housebound for almost five days and was feeling a mite better. And I am, arguably, a bit of a showboat. The other three writers read well-written, meaningful material. I presented a six-year-old performance piece that, whilst well-received, was essentially creative trivia. I may have also given someone the flu. I don't know for sure if I did but guilt is like that. It creeps its way into your mind and convinces you of whatever it is you feel the need to be convinced about. My real or imagined guilt for attending the gathering was negated by my descent into my new guilty, no matter real or imagined, Typhoid Mary status. That's the thing about guilt; it's like the Blob (that old Steve McQueen movie,) it reproduces itself like crazy.

As it was, my sense of well-being lasted about the length of the meeting. I came home, had a jigger of curative brandy and was smoothly swallowed back into the belly of the flu beast. *"We gather our arms full of guilt as though it were precious stuff. It must be that we want it that way."* ~ **John Steinbeck**

The next day, I began to pay the price. This particular flu seemed centered in my chest, an always vulnerable part of my aging and clearly disintegrating body. As a youthful non-voting member of the military industrial complex, I contracted pneumonia. My lungs since have never been 100%.

As for the re-emergence of my treasured virus, about the only saving grace I could find was that the Australian Open had begun and I enjoyed many feverish moments of entertainment, spectating tennis played during an excruciating heat wave.

Meanwhile, the first obligation of the week that went into the tank was the regular DIRA meeting. I am one of a few stalwart band of Islanders who still attend DIRA meetings. Many good citizens have opted to stay away, to forsake this middle-aged forum of debate and egalitarian endurance. Why they have chosen to let this monthly round-table of democratic discourse wither on the vine of invisibility is beyond me.

Some of our citizenry have never even *tasted* the fruit of the DIRA tree. Either they are too busy to test the waters *(my metaphors are getting feverishly awkward, aren't they?)* or, more likely, they have dismissed it on the advice of their political prophets, an especially prevalent category of seer on Denman.

As ignored as DIRA generally is, forty folks did attend the January 13th meeting that focused on our beloved ferry system. I fear that the end result of that meeting, and two bits, would have, once upon a time, bought you a cup of coffee. *"If you've had the right kind of education, it's amazing how many things*

185

you can find to feel guilty about." ~ **Pete McCarthy: A Journey of Discovery in Ireland**

Tuesday, I was scheduled to attend the monthly meeting of the Arts Denman Board. It is an incongruously structured duck. Only the four-person executive actually vote. The balance of the Board represents a comfortable conspiracy of various branches of the local artis-tree. I have only been attending since the Audio Arts Collective decided to go legit. This would be the second meeting in a row I had backed out of.

Wednesday, my most important meeting of the week was also on the scratch list. I have spent the past year on the Board of the Denman Health Centre Society. Our AGM would usually be a little attended affair and Board members should really try and make these annual accountings. On the other hand, sick people should avoid them like the plague. If last year's attendance is a predictor, most Denman Islanders will stay home, maybe with the flu; perhaps with a dollop of guilt.

The absence of attendance at the Clinic AGM is not the same as missing a DIRA meeting. While DIRA has been actively, and quite carelessly, tossed aside by many, most Islanders likely have no comprehensive understanding of how their Clinic operates. One has to admire this obliviousness.

Thursday, the monthly Audio Arts Open Stage rolled around. I had already planted the seed for begging off and my participation has been minimal over the past few months. My absence was barely noticed. Apparently it was one of our best. Drat! *"When they call the roll in the Senate, the Senators do not know whether to answer 'Present' or 'Not guilty.'"* ~ **Theodore Roosevelt**

My flu lingers. By mid-February this yoyo virus has come and gone a number of times. I could go to the Doctor but I still hope to recover by outlasting it. This attempt at medicinal indolence has worked for me in the past. And I am not alone. Many friends and acquaintances have been holed up for weeks, snivelling and hacking their hearts out. My guilt has lessened, however. It's heartening to have recovered from *something.*

Belonging

"I don't even remember the season. I just remember walking between them and feeling for the first time that I belonged somewhere." ~ **Stephen Chbosky, The Perks of Being a Wallflower**

On the first day of the Sochi Olympics, and the day after an ardent protest of the apparently deteriorating conditions at the Denman Island Community School, I felt compelled to begin to make some observations about welcoming and belonging and other experiences of inclusion or, naturellement, exclusion.

In the larger world, there is no event comparable to the Olympics. In 2014, this particular sporting extravaganza presented new and not so fresh challenges to all concerned. For example, to create the infrastructure for Sochi, countless residents were relocated. Many of those displaced left their dogs behind. When reporters covering the Olympics first arrived at Sochi, mutts were all over the place, welcoming visitors because dogs, except for junk yard dogs and the like, generally *are* welcoming. The dogs of Sochi belonged there and, like good hosts, were simultaneously lost and looking for love. The Russian Olympic hierarchy would not likely have desired such a sad residue of their forced removal policies. Nevertheless, it was an inevitable by-product of massive Olympian excess. For me, it hammered home a point; to belong and be lost at the same time is a wretched condition. *"Some of us aren't meant to belong. Some of us have to turn the world upside down and shake the hell out of it until we make our own place in it."* ~ **Elizabeth Lowell, Author**

Forced relocation and residential disruption seems to be a perennial outcome for such massive events.

The newer, more overt Putin-escan twist for Sochi, one that has existed somewhat in the shadows, has rarely seen such global light *(or darkness)*, was the purposefully provocative Russian anti-gay legislation. Tolerance and acceptance for LGBT citizens of the world has increased considerably in the past few years, albeit not with the speed many rightly would want. Nevertheless, even as the Olympic movement touted the community of the world and the beauty of sport, repression in some baleful quarters multiplied. More pronounced, as a few commentators noted, the athletic participants at Sochi failed to make even one public political expression of disgust or remorse. *"I been with strangers all day and they treated me like family. I come in here to family and you treat me like a stranger."* ~ **August Wilson, Author**

When I consider my adopted community, I think, 'A reasonably good place to live.' I think, 'There is tolerance here.' I think, 'There is *some* diversity here.' But I also think a heretical thought, 'Denman is like many places.' There are petty jealousies and bullying *(a term that sporadically gets tossed around like confetti at a wedding)* and social structures that can seem stratified, molded, fired hard *(yet brittle)* like clay. While there is a wealth of life-styles here, there is, from my experience, a restricted willingness to self-examine, to look with a practiced and critical eye at our collective shortcomings. On the contrary, there is, sometimes, a surplus of sycophancy, glad-handing and neighbourly group think.

Although burdened with deeply held hermit tendencies, I come at the conundrum of living in a rather loosely structured collective from the perspective of a reasonably active and engaged participant in the life of my community. Even without many musical proclivities, I have *always* found myself prone to *"travel to the beat of a different drum"* even before I heard Linda Ronstadt and the Stone Poneys sing Michael Nesmith's harmonious anthem.

This predisposition to favour insular endeavours has simultaneously allowed me to mostly maintain my own counsel and, in candid moments, lament my less engaging behaviour and, on occasion, those of others. *"I didn't belong as a kid, and that always bothered me. If only I'd known that one day my differentness would be an asset, then my early life would have been much easier."* ~ **Bette Midler**

I would have strenuously avoided publicly commenting on the recent situation at the Community School *except* for the sign *'Fire the Principal'*. For a brief time during the affair, others slap-dashedly tossed around names, positions and apparent motives and characteristics of key players as if they were actors on Coronation Street, or The Guiding Light *(neither of which I have ever seen)*. A couple of more contemplative electronic observers opined that perhaps processes and privacy should be respected. I heartily endorsed that perspective from the bleachers.

However, at some point in the energetic farce, a forester, or some otherwise high-wire artiste, erected a homemade sign *(etched with doodled flower and a few hearts)* that declared *(without the benefit of a referendum)* **Denman Island says Fire the Principal Save our loving school.** He, she or they hung this hastily wrought homage high on the barren, almost naked Denman Tree Post and then scurried away to their underutilized art studio. The sign hung there for a few weeks. No one mentioned it. For a time, the perfectly innocent DIRA meeting signpost was an unfortunate companion.

Twice I drew the 'Fire the Principal' sign to the attention of acquaintances to gauge opinion. One day the sign was gone. Before long the whole bumptious tableau was absorbed into the humdrum of the everyday. There may or there may not be long-term fallout from the school skirmish. Life seems to be going on. As is Denman's habit, not much will change although there are always small adjustments. School Boards around the province are facing incredible fiscal challenges. School dustups are legion. ***"I'm a satirist, so I've got boxing gloves on if the person is worthy of satire. But I'm not an assassin."*** ~ **Stephen Colbert**

Some might say, 'This particular incident is over. Why on earth bring it up again? To what end?' In my ideal world, most everything should be discussed. Events *need* light. To plan for the future, as much as one can, there needs to be a rational process to examine the past with the lustre of questions. Thus far, I have seen little luminosity on the examining table of Denman. Reason suggests that we talk about it, whatever *it* is. Picking *it* apart analytically, satirizing *it* if necessary *(it is almost always necessary in my book)* and ultimately, coming to terms with it all. Whether the ethical and social residue of the **Hot, Cool, Yours** Olympics or the heated flurry of action that rose up on Denman in February will ever really get talked out, I feel a public duty to myself, if no one else, to make note of both.

"Volun-tears" - I'll Cry Tomorrow...I'm Too Busy Right Now

"Research has shown that people who volunteer often live longer." ~ **Allen Klein**

Not so long ago, on a gloomy, foggy winter morn *(as opposed to those all too infrequently bright and bubbly foggy winter morns, I suppose)*, I began this essay on the perils of volunteerism. As for why I thought there were any perils to be found, I need to be clear that I *do* volunteer, have volunteered much of my life. None of that prepared me for my move to Denman Island and the demands that ooze for volunteers on this Island.

Even before I had permanently moved here *(which, for the record, was at Christmas, 2003)* I had been dragooned by the then dynamic DIRA press gang, a Denman process partially replacing the more traditional Welcome Wagon 'howdy". My immersion into the diluted DIRA swimming pool was a relatively painless textbook transition. The result, though, *(and DIRA just happened to be the first to snap me up, prize package that I am)* was to propel me sideways and induce me to spend the rest of my productive *(and likely a goodly number of my unproductive)* years on committees. *"Here's to all volunteers, those dedicated people who believe in all work and no pay."* ~ **Robert Orben**

Board work! Bored work, a witless wag might reply! You see where I am going with this, right? I lament that there may not be an original board bone-picking thingamabob in my body. I *am* but a lowly mirror of the struggles many experience to replenish their sparse Board larder.

For example, how often have you heard *(or spoken)* this uplifting chant? *'You can count on me... as long as I don't have to sit on a committee.'* Or, *'I really want to help, but I'm totally not a Board person.'* One always has to admire such trenchant honesty. Really, very few of us are suited to the rigours of serving on a Board. Some relent, of course. *'Okay,'* a few might allow, *'I will sit on your Board, as long as I don't have to do anything.'*

Most volunteer Board recruiters breathe a sigh of relief at having reached this tipping point. *'I've got you now,'* they quietly note, with just a twinge of guilt, *'welcome aboard the good ship We-Really-Need-Someone-Who-Knows-Their-Limitations-But-Brings-At-Least-A-Thimbleful-Of-Enthusiasm.'*

'Hold your horses,' I hear you say. *'Why are you slagging people who only want to help?'* No slag is intended. Honest! What *is* intended is to draw to the attention of the few who might happen to read this *(I say 'the few' because there is the perception in some circles that very few people read the Flagstone, though I wonder how anyone could resist its engaging draw)* about what I consider an obvious 'most revolting state of affairs'. To paraphrase Teddy Roosevelt, and maybe Art Carney's alter ego, Ed Norton: 'Uncle Sam needs YOU!'. Okay, perhaps that is too off-center and jingoistic. Still, the point is, as schlocky as it sounds, DENMAN NEEDS VOLUNTEERS as much as, if not more than, MARS NEEDS WOMEN. *"No, no! I said Volunteering -- NOT Orienteering! Now we're in the middle of nowhere.... and just who's gonna pay the price for getting us out of this mess?"* ~ **Anonymous**

As is my custom with the concoction of my Gentrified Soul compositions, I sought out half a dozen funny and/or pungent quotes to riff off, to help focus and structure my acerbic commentary. It is also, as must be evident by now, a cheap trick I overuse. People might not want to read *me* but they might just want to read quotes from the famous. This article has quoted only one modest celebrity. I won't embarrass you by pointing out *his* quote just in case his name is unfamiliar to you.

While there were a few *nearly* humorous quotes to be found in cyberspace, no doubt most contributed by quote volunteers who spent every waking hour posting them out on the internet, none immediately screamed, *'Funny!'*

Many were saccharine in the extreme. They seemed to have been concocted with one fundamental intent; to promote volunteerism as a religious experience where, evidently, any rewards to be had will be found, if not in heaven, then in the smiles of the eternally grateful. Such is the lot of the poor volunteer; their ultimate reward will be found in volunteer Valhalla. *"Working in an underdeveloped land for two or three years, the volunteer will often find that his work is routine and full of frustration."* ~ **Sargent Shriver**

There are, for my vague purposes and from my vast experience, five main types of volunteers.

- Leaders who love to guide others and over-function brilliantly, not unlike the energizer bunny;
- Former leaders who understand how odious unrestrained leadership can be and practice it sparingly, if at all;
- Former followers who used to occasionally guide others but found the whole thing uncomfortable and now take the long way around to avoid the quicksand of local volunteerism;
- Leaders who specialize in short-term projects which they can control so they won't get sucked into ongoing demands;
- Most everyone else who has the time and the interest and steps up.

As you can see, this totally spurious sampling presupposes that almost EVERYONE has been a leader, or been led, somewhere. My completely unscientific supposition is that many of my gentry conspirators who have travelled to this little Island *(and of course, elsewhere, where the issues are not dissimilar)* played some sort of leadership/follower role. The world is full of people aging and living on the fruits of their past laurels. If we succeeded in our previous incarnation, the odds are that the skills we once used will transfer easily to this little hunk of rock.

If only, eh!

"Volunteering: we don't pay, so no, you can't quit." ~ **Apparently an anonymous twitter thought**

Afterword

This meandering exposition has tried to come to grips with the scourge of diminishing volunteers that I sense *(and others might well acknowledge)* exists on this Island. Many of the traditional *(and a number of upstart)* organizations are predominantly the domain of the 'older' demographic. A few are clearly emerging for the 'likely-inevitably-doomed-to-age-rapidly' demographic, a small number to be sure, many who seem to me to be singularly unimpressed by traditional organizations. Additionally, some of those community members who have volunteered over the past forty years are more discerning with their available remaining hours. They have 'done their time' and are happily enjoying an extended parole.

There are exceptions to this rule, of course.

As this article imprecisely wraps up, I would like to praise the volunteer efforts of one and all. Volunteers not only bring their skills and interests to the tasks at hand, they also develop additional skills. Healthy organizations need to identify the skills and talents they do need and, if there is a deficit, find ways to assist volunteers to gain the needed tools. I sincerely hope my rough-edged juvenile satire hasn't impacted volunteers negatively.

I would have preferred to end my Gentrified Soul series on a more humorous note. Alas, on any given day, humour is either there, or it isn't. I began this final column not actually knowing that it would be my last in this series. I have decided that I have other writing fish to fry. There is no more sizzle here.

Adieu.

Bill Engleson Autobiography

On the day I was born, or thereabouts, my parents pulled into a dock at Powell River and made their way to the hospital.

I am pretty sure it went that way. They never actually spelled out the details and I never asked. I can't imagine we lingered more than a couple of days in that seaside town after I was delivered.

The next year and a half was spent on their fish boat. I am told I developed sea legs. I assume that is true. I never fell into the chuck. They never mentioned it anyways. We finally came to shore in Nanaimo. A Pulp Mill had to be built. My father signed on.

I came of age in Nanaimo. In my later teens, I left, had a truncated Canadian military encounter in Kingston, a tail-between-my-legs return to High School to repeat Grade 12 (after signing a behavioural contract,) and a second, more permanent exit into my own wonky version of maturity and liberation.

I attended SFU as a charter student, dropped out whilst remaining within, immersed myself in student politics, had a six-month flirtation with Frontier College and spent more than a decade living in the CRCA, a New Westminster Co-op/Commune which is celebrating its Fiftieth Anniversary in August, 2017.

For a career, I spent twenty-four years with MCFD, initially as a family support worker and, post-Solidarity, 1983, as a child protection social worker. In 2002, I accepted early retirement but after a couple of months of mind-numbing sloth, went to work, for one and a half years, with the Lower Mainland Purpose Society headquartered in New Westminster. Previously I had served on the Board of Directors for many years.

All along the plan, our post-work life plan, was for my partner and I to live in the country, preferably on an Island. Devil's Island or Denman Island. It didn't matter. Well, it mattered some. Life on Denman has been full, mostly with writing, volunteering, table tennis and, of late, Pickleball.

To keep as active as is befitting a retired social worker who writes, I maintain a blog, www.engleson.ca, and occasionally post both musings on writing and observations on the state of Child Welfare.

There is an intensity to rural life yet, all the while, a comfortable detachment exists; can exist. The community struggles, yet comes together.

I like to think my writing hasn't hindered its intermittent coalescence.

-

Author Profile

Bill Engleson's first novel *"Like a Child to Home" (2013 Friesen Press)* tells the story of an older child welfare Social Worker, Wally Rose, the system he works in, the youth he services, and the complexity of the world with which they all struggle. This novel is concerned with child protection and children in care in British Columbia. It attempts to accurately portray aspects of the provision of child welfare from the perspective of an everyday social worker.

Bill is working on a number of projects including a prequel to *"Like a Child to Home"* entitled *"Drawn Towards the Sun"*; a mystery, *"Bloodhound Days"*; and another collection of home-grown, satirically-tinged essays, *"DIRA Diary: Tall Tales of Democracy in Traction."*

His poetry and fiction have appeared in *"Minus Tides International"*; and a somewhat delayed, hopefully forthcoming, anthology of poetry, *"Words Fly Away,"* honouring Fukushima: https://fukushimapoetry.wordpress.com/

He was included in the recent Comox Valley Writers Society Centennial Anthology, *"Writers & Books - Comox Valley 1865-2015"*